Why Family Therapy Doesn't Work And What We Can Do About It

Adventures In Family Based Therapy

By

Nancy Marshall, M.A.

ISBN: 1-4140-5785-7 (e-book)
ISBN: 1-4140-5784-9 (Paperback)

Library of Congress Control Number: 2004090201

This book is printed on acid free paper.

Printed in the United States of America
Bloomington, IN

1stBooks – rev. 02/10/04

TABLE OF CONTENTS

FOREWARD

I wrote this book because I don't think people understand what is happening to them emotionally. If they don't succeed in therapy, individually or as a family, they feel ashamed and afraid. Clinicians say it's their fault; they are "too sick to be helped."

I hope this book clarifies what we are all up against and gives some good techniques for working with it.

I hope also that the book can help dedicated young clinicians who would like to be really effective, because being really effective can be so satisfying. It is THE prevention for burnout.

This book is dedicated to all of those people who have tried to love someone else and found it difficult.

INTRODUCTION

Throughout my years as a therapist, I have learned that the most deeply-rooted fears of an individual of any age must be calmed, otherwise he or she will never be able to deal successfully with another person. The fears can be hidden, "gated away" by the brain to protect itself. Often the client himself may not even realize the extent to which fears are driving everyday behavior. It is the therapist's job to coax these fears into the open and calm them.

All behavior is goal oriented; people are trying to achieve something. Behavior is a form of interpersonal negotiation. Under normal circumstances this is o.k., but sometimes these negotiations and behaviors can take some very odd and unsuccessful approaches.

For example, a deep lack of self-confidence could cause a spouse, or a parent, to present anything of importance to another family member in a scolding and shaming manner, perhaps because this person has deeply embedded fears about not being taken seriously or not being an important person. The "scolder/shamer" may have fears of abandonment if he is not in control, and the scolding or shaming style of interaction assures him that he has attained the status of an important person and that he will be taken seriously, i.e., the much-desired control. The fears are deeply embedded. There is no value in trying to teach the "scolder" to communicate. He is communicating. Nor does the other family member need to learn to adjust to the scolding. Effective treatment can calm both individuals so that they can successfully negotiate with each other and get their needs met without using coercion or capitulating to the will of another in a way that breeds resentment.

There are two main causes of failure in therapy. Many treatments just recreate the old arguments and have the clients argue in front of the therapist. The therapist fills the role of "teacher" and the clients vie to tell on one another and "be right". The key fears of the clients must be rooted out and calmed. If they are not, in spite of any communication "rules" given, when the stress becomes high enough, each client will revert to old behavior, the same behavior that brought them into therapy in the first place.

The second cause of failure is fairly simple. The efforts to change the mind, calm the fears, have not been applied with enough determination and the effort has not been consistent enough. People often give up just short of a real healing.

Our wonderful minds are very much things of habit. We think what we have thought before. To change any habit requires a very determined effort. I once heard the process of changing beliefs compared to the task of moving the position of a huge ocean liner. The boat is very heavy, thus there is huge inertia. Tug boats push from all sides. The tides may shift, again causing the liner to shift, perhaps not in the desired direction. Again and again, I used to watch this process from my apartment in New York, which overlooked the Hudson River docks. Impatience could bring disaster: a precipitous crash into the dock. Consistent, patient effort was the only way to get the ocean liner into the slip. It also takes consistent, patient effort to change one's beliefs.

This is not necessarily a plea for a long time in treatment. In my experience, effective therapy will begin to take hold, and move a person's beliefs within three months of regular visits. Treatment may not be complete in three months, but some beginning shifts in attitude and behavior should appear if treatment reaches the deep core beliefs and fears. If the deep fears of the person are not reached, change will not appear.

Serious fears are firmly bound even within body tissues and they exist on a level well below reason. Therapists monitoring quarrels between clients can see the heavy breathing, raised voices and rapid vocal cadence, and even reddened faces. Clients will report upset stomachs, racing hearts, and tightened muscles. Many modern therapists feel memory, or a form of it, may be stored in body tissues and not relegated to the brain only; and therefore, many current therapies make an effort to deal with the body and move away from simply "chatting" with the client.

Well-intentioned therapists cannot rationally ask people not to be afraid. I can imagine disgruntled clients hearing therapists' pleas that must sound very smug, thinking, "Yeah, well I already THOUGHT OF THAT. I JUST CAN'T DO IT. Thanks for nothing."

Interactions with parents and children and between spouses are activating deep fears within each individual. Again, that very scolding, shaming person may fear being abandoned, or fear he or she is not worthy of being listened to, which causes the inappropriate behavior. As the interaction intensifies, so do the fears which are tapping into old memories of being abandoned or discounted. These fears must be calmed before interpersonal negotiations can reasonably continue.

This is why so many people hate to be in marital therapy. The fears are repeatedly stirred, often with no resolution. The "scolding" person feels more afraid than ever, and now is additionally shamed by having the behavior seen by a stranger (the therapist). In essence, each person can be retraumatized in each session. Some group therapies also stir fears without resolving them, also retraumatizing clients. I met an older clinician at a Veteran's Administration hospital who turned to EMDR, Eye Movement Desensitization and Reprocessing, almost exclusively and worked with clients individually at the hospital in Philadelphia before he put them into group therapy. He didn't want them retraumatizing each other.

Intellect and emotion are created by separate neural systems, and this is the cause of the seeming disconnect between feelings and reason. The limbic, primitive brain is common to all mammals; emotions, hormones and all instincts are lodged in it. Because of this, we see some very stupid decisions made by people we regard as usually intelligent.

Attitudes take serious remedial work. Asking people to communicate is very popular in therapy. It will not do the job. THEY ARE COMMUNICATING. People are always communicating through their actions. Even not communicating is communicating. Either the partner is afraid the communication won't be accepted, or he or she doesn't have enough respect for the other to BOTHER communicating. Many times the client wants the therapist to scare or shame the partner (or child) into communicating something different.

Deep limbic system issues will not go away because the therapist intellectually points them out, no matter how engaging or insightful the personality of the therapist.

When doing marital and family therapy, the initial session should assess the nature of complaints each has about the other. The clients should then be separated for the purpose of reducing each individual's fears. Only then is there efficacy in rejoining them. Only then can strategic family therapy help the family.

This book will discuss the ways in which the fears affect the person's relationship to his family and to society. The fears form problematical core beliefs which affect his or her choices of behavior across all areas in his or her life. They have been formed throughout the individual's lifetime by a type of empirical testing and evaluating system. What is this world really like? Am I safe in it? What is the best way for me to navigate this world with the abilities that I have?

An initial assessment should be done. If clients have their motivation and forces of will in agreement with the goal of working together, remedial individual work should be done for several months.
Only then can the family unit be rejoined in therapy for negotiation.

CHAPTER ONE: WHAT IS FAMILY-BASED THERAPY?

In 1984, the federal government developed a new initiative for counseling of troubled families. Before that time, the drug culture and continuing difficult cultural values caused a "boom" in institutional and foster care placement of children. Suddenly, very large numbers of children were placed outside of their families. The outcomes following these placements were not good. Some studies conducted in the Midwest found that a high percentage of homeless people had grown up in the foster care system. The placement systems are quite expensive to governments in addition to yielding poor results in terms of individuals with self-efficacy.

It was decided to move from the old autocratic model of treatment into something more collaborative and to attempt to empower and heal the family in its own environment. Preserving the original family, where the bonds lay, was decided to be the best way to help vulnerable children.

Dr. Marion Lindblad-Goldberg discussed home-based treatment in her excellent book, Creating Competence From Chaos. "...the 1984 federal CASSP initiative was interpreted in Pennsylvania as an opportunity to develop a shared belief system and collaborative partnership among the child-serving systems –namely, mental health, child welfare, mental retardation, juvenile justice, drug and alcohol, education, health care, and vocational rehabilitation."

CASSP stands for Child Adolescent Service Support System. It works well in Pennsylvania, where I practice. Instead of one official, social worker, making choices about a child's needs, a team is assembled from all of the various systems. The child himself and the family must be represented in meetings. Strengths are looked for and family resources of various sorts are encouraged. The cultural beliefs of the family should be considered. Any type of treatment should be periodically evaluated by this team so that no one is operating in a vacuum and to ensure that the family feels respected and "heard".

Nancy Marshall, M.A.

References

Lindblad-Goldberg, M. et. al. (1998). <u>Creating Competence From Chaos.</u> New York:
W.W. Norton and Company.

CHAPTER TWO: BEGIN WITH A GOOD ASSESSMENT

Before treatment can proceed, it is essential for a clinician to really understand what is happening in the family. Amazingly, this step is sometimes skipped over and therapists attempt to pick up the information over time. This is a serious error. People are complicated. Things are not always what they seem to be; people don't even know the truths about what they are themselves doing in some cases. No responsible medical doctor would begin treatment of an internal illness without really understanding the disease. Nor should mental health professionals.

Each family member should be given the opportunity to relate or present a good history. Especially important is how each family member has found interpersonal experiences to be. How the original family treated each other; his, her original family should be closely examined. Find out from the client who he could go to as a child with fears; with accomplishments. What responses were received? Any traumas and abuses should be examined. At what ages did these things happen? We weather events differently at age two than we do at age sixteen. Or thirty. How well we weather events is greatly affected by the interpersonal support we enjoy. The therapist should attempt to determine a "base line" sense of the individual's general resilience. We vary greatly in our resilience.

Clients need privacy. Always interview family members individually, at least for part of the interviews. Children should never listen to very difficult parental histories. It is too frightening, too stimulating, and even too disheartening for children to hear them.

One of the very largest failings of contemporary society is that children do not experience sheltered years. They are wise and cynical without understanding and context. Children understand complex adult situations in a surface manner only. Events can feel very frightening to them, and they do not have a good understanding of the resources people possess which can assist them in dealing with the events.   They adopt a smug cynicism which is really a mask for anxiety and fear.

Assess whether the family is using common sense in sheltering children in family therapy. Telephone conversations and television programs are frequently overheard by children when they should not be. Recently I was working with a woman who had experienced two miscarriages and was again pregnant. She feared losing the baby, and thus was very unwilling to tell her eleven-year-old daughter that she was pregnant. Yet she was having telephone quarrels with the baby's father concerning his demands that she get an abortion, and his reluctance to pay child support. All of this was taking place in a very tiny living space, where the eleven year old could easily overhear the conflict.

Television programs and movies should be monitored. I have often been in homes in which three-year-olds were wandering around, idly viewing horror movies. This is begging for unnecessary trouble. Most parents would not stuff fetid garbage into their child's mouth, but the airwaves and the Internet are allowed to bring it into the home daily. Children are very busy forming a philosophy of life as they study the environment. I did not allow my daughter to view violent images even at fourteen or fifteen years of age. She complained at length, and undoubtedly snuck such films at times, but I did what I could as a parent. Even now, at my age, I myself avoid negative stimulating images. Try to assess the emotional climate in the home, including what friends and relatives visit, what they say, and what stimulating media images are permitted.

People in assessment may gloss over the seriousness of any abuses or parental neglect they suffered. They may truly have this information "gated" away from consciousness, they may feel shame they were treated in this way, or they may be making a valiant effort to put it behind them or to protect the reputation of their parents.

If a client becomes reticent during the assessment, respect him and step back a little, but take note of the reticence and return to that area in subsequent sessions. If a client becomes angry or teary during the assessment, he has given you both a gift. You now know what is a painful area and what the client feels about it. You know right where to begin the treatment.

Be sure to look at peer interaction when assessing children. Peer and sibling relationships, unfortunately, can engender significant trauma. Schools are typically not able to monitor much of what takes place in peer groups.

Help the client look for his Core Beliefs. Always name it for what it is, and confront it. Follow the "arrow" downward to find the belief, because many statements the client will make reveal beliefs. "I'm a failure" means WHAT about the client's core beliefs?

Look at Inhibitions

A simple checklist gives a clinician a good indicator of the client's condition. Is the client too easily shocked, too fear laden? Is he too timid and does he fear rejection too much? When I treated teenagers at a drug and alcohol rehabilitation hospital, many were not able to simply look at their own eyes in a mirror reflection. They felt such a dislike of themselves, and a deeply embedded shame, even claiming their own mirror images was difficult.

Ask the client to consider whether these responses differ at home from those in public:
Can the client dance?
Can he shout?
Can he tell a joke?
Is he able to accept a compliment?
Can he admit he is wrong?
Can he express emotion?
Can he allow himself to express a divergent opinion from another?
Can he apologize?
Can the client read aloud or speak to a group?

The most flexible person is the most secure person. A person with too many inhibitions may live a dull life and never achieve his full potential.

Ask the client to complete the thought:
People like me because_____.
People dislike me because_____.
People expect me to_____.
I control myself by_____.
I need_____.
I hate_____.
I can't_____.
I'm afraid that_____.
I love_____.
I worry about_____.

Develop a working hypothesis of what is happening with family members. Don't be afraid to alter your hypothesis as new information is revealed. Clinicians should be nothing if not flexible in their thinking. I used to compare assessment to putting together a very elaborate and difficult 1, 000-piece puzzle. For hours, various sections seem unrelated. Finally, as pieces are joined together it becomes clear, oh, this is the horse, that is a section of bushes, etc. Families and their unspoken agreements can be complicated. Don't be afraid to discard theories and keep looking for answers.

PART ONE: WHAT HAS HAPPENED

CHAPTER THREE: THE BRAIN DEALING WITH STRESS

With a sudden stress, or chronic negative conditions, the sympathetic nervous system activates the release of adrenaline. The animal is preparing for fight or flight. Blood leaves the brain and goes to muscles, the eyes may dilate and fixate. The heartbeat rate increases. The animal breathes differently, more rapidly, or perhaps more haltingly. The animal is focused on survival and the thinking process is not complex at that time.

The increase in adrenaline is toxic to the body and must be cleaned out by the liver. Adrenaline changes the cells of the body and lowers immune system functioning. If adrenaline is in the body on a chronic basis it lowers levels of the hormone dopamine and the person will seem hyperactive.

If this hormone crisis continues, the animal's body will release morphine. This means nature is regarding there may be an injury to the body. This morphine will cause the animal to feel "spacey".

We are seeing exactly this type of appearance and behavior in adults and children who have had had a serious exposure to a traumatic event, or who are chronically feeling threatened. My years as a therapist have taught me that people are very sensitive, both in body and mind, and what appears to be a small challenge or a small stress to another person may not be so small to a particular child or adult.

We are now seeing that unpleasant memories are encoded in the entire body. Massage therapists have noted that deep tissue work in an area can sometimes release a mysterious flood of anger or sadness. The new psychotherapies that involve the body almost always see changes in the client's body while working with traumatic memories. Clients may experience pressure in their stomachs, in their shoulders, and areas around the heart may ache. Treatments like Eye Movement Desensitization and Reprocessing (EMDR), which will be further discussed in this book, give us an ability to examine the memories and have the person re-experience them to end the sensitivity to them.

Unresolved stress acts as a "ticking time bomb" and will cause physical difficulty and will drive odd behavior. People will make some adaptation to powerful stimuli, and it may be a maladaptation: too much personal aggression, an inappropriate timidity, self-medication with drugs and alcohol, the maladaptations are as myriad and varied as are people themselves. The challenge in therapy is to find and identify the original stimuli, reduce and reprocess the response to it, and help the person to stop continuously responding to the dead past and the imagined future and be fully alive-in the right now:

"Over the years, the mind is diminished more and more because the blockage of emotional energy is intensified EACH TIME A SIMILAR EXPERIENCE OCCURS. Every time we have a new experience that is in any way similar to the original trauma, we feel an intensity that is disproportionate to what is actually going on. I referred to this earlier as spontaneous age regression.

"The wounded inner child is filled with unresolved energy resulting from the sadness of childhood trauma. One of the reasons we have sadness is to complete painful events of the past so that our energy can be available for the present. When we are not allowed to grieve, the energy is frozen" (Bradshaw, 1990, p. 61).

Clinicians have theorized that limbic system structures can become increasingly sensitized and the person then is in a chronic central sympathetic system arousal. Anything that reminds the individual of a former trauma can set off a kind of neural "kindling" and this creates a stability for Post Traumatic Stress Disorder (PTSD), which, if untreated, will affect the person for decades.

Francine Shapiro, the psychologist who developed EMDR, refers to painful events as being dysfunctionally stored in the brain. I explain to clients that because some events are very painful, and feel unresolved, the brain will ruminate, or go over and over, the events in a vain effort at resolution. They need to be "coaxed out" by a technique like EMDR or Thought Field Therapy. This will be discussed more fully in the section on Treatment.

In the year 2000, three M.D.s from California, Dr. Thomas Lewis, Dr. Fari Amini, and Dr. Richard Lannon, produced a very interesting book called <u>A General Theory of Love.</u> Their purpose was to explain an age-old mystery, why one falls in love with a particular individual. Their book is fascinating in and of itself, but it also does a good job in explaining the ancient, emotional brain and its nervous system. This limbic system actually drives our behavior, and, if we're lucky, there is some mediation of behavior by our more developed cognitive brains. Doctors Lewis, Amini and Lannon describe the effects of poor nurturing on the developing child. Their book helps clarify how deeply damage flows.

Dr. Bessel van der Kolk is probably the world's foremost expert in trauma. He compares PTSD to a variation of human stress arousal. Understanding PTSD helps explain very odd behavior: "The 'Stockholm Syndrome, ' sometimes found among hostages, is a case in point. The name derives from the case of a Stockholm bank robbery in which several of the hostages captured during the holdup defended their captor when released. It is now used to describe the alignment of positive affections by hostages toward their captors. Although typically explained via the psychoanalytic concepts of identification with the aggressor, it seems possible that the victims' needs for a stable conceptual system may play a role in this phenomenon as well. By regarding their captors positively, hostages are able to maintain a belief in a benevolent environment in which their own safety and security are maximized. Their situation appears relatively benign, thereby minimizing the terror associated with their predicament" (van der Kolk, 1987, p. 80).

How very much this also describes many marriages and many childhoods in American life. We are very fortunate to live in an era that utilizes many good affective therapy techniques, for it is the affective (limbic) systems that must be reached. Hypnotherapy is a good technique, as are EMDR and Thought Field Therapy. Some gestalt work and strategic family work can reach the limbic system.

Traditional play therapy for children, music, drawing and painting can be of value. In my opinion, however, the EMDR and Thought Field work move a client more rapidly than any other techniques.

In response to stress, endorphins are released in the brain. As the endorphins wear off an unpleasant sensation which feels almost like an opiate withdrawal may takes place. The person may actually reintroduce stress unconsciously to again experience the endorphin release. The behavior will look very destructive to the person's peers. It is a type of trauma re-enactment. Good affective therapy must be done.

We also see many abused or traumatized clients with anhedonia, or an inability to experience pleasure. It is concomitant to depression and trauma. It is especially sad to see a young person express in a "flat" way and be unable to enjoy ordinary pleasures of life. Affective therapy will help and some good modeling can help the client. Therapists who are able to work out in the field can create fun-filled adventures and take the client along for the "ride." Modeling must be done in tandem with the affective treatments in order to be effective, however.

To only work with the rational, cognitive approaches is like clicking open the wrong folder on the computer desktop. It won't access the material wanted. You have an open folder, but it's the wrong folder. In Woody Allen's movies he jokes about being in therapy for decades with no result. Good therapy that is sufficiently challenging to the client should begin to move him along, yielding some behavioral changes within three months.

As stated, A General Theory of Love gives us a very clear picture of limbic system connections and what results we can see in the person's life when the limbic system is responding with too much amplitude for the situation at hand: "[The] purpose of the limbic brain was to monitor the external world and the internal bodily environment, and to orchestrate their congruence. What one sees, hears, feels, and smells is fed into the limbic brain, and so is data about bodily temperature, blood pressure, heart rate, digestive processes, and scores of other somatic parameters. The limbic brain stands at the convergence of these two information streams; it coordinates them and fine-tunes physiology to prime the body for the outside world" (Lewis et. al., 2000, p. 32).

Others have said it's the job of the brain to keep the body alive. The limbic system quickly fields data and the environment. How safe is this mammal? Does he need to take action? Many of the bodily processes work in an automatic, interlocking manner and we need never be aware of them. We also look at other mammals in the environment.

The limbic system is also our mediator in interpersonal matters: "The limbic brain evaluates the nature of the other's intentions-is it careless, aggressive, friendly, sexual, submissive, indifferent?

"Once the limbic brain has settled on an emotional state, it sends outputs to the neocortical brain, spawning a conscious thought (Who the hell does this guy think he is?)" (Lewis et. al., 2000, p. 33)

The doctors have good senses of humor, but they are telling us that the primitive brain makes the first evaluation of the other. This limbic system evaluation then moves out into the more recently developed cortical thinking areas and we gives names and categories and form opinions about what we have just experienced.

The doctors agree, the neocortical (thinking) brain is the "wrong folder", as therapist Dr. John Omaha puts it, for emotional thoughts: "Because the last brain in the evolutionary sequence directs the abstract mind, we must credit the neocortex for the towering human achievements in cognition-language, problem-solving physics, mathematics. Emotional function doesn't require many hypotheticals-it takes neocortical genius to formulate the theory of relativity, but not to be sad after a loss, or to be thrilled at seeing the person you love across a crowded room" (Lewis et. al., 2000, p. 56).

The ways in which we relate to others are very profoundly mediated in the limbic system:

"Take a puppy away from his mother, place him alone in a wicker pen, and you will witness the universal mammalian reaction to the rupture of an attachment bond-a reflection of the limbic architecture mammals share. Short separations provoke an acute response known as PROTEST while prolonged separations yield the physiologic state of DESPAIR.

"Human adults exhibit a protest response as much as any other mammal. Anyone who has been jilted in an infatuation (i.e., just about everybody) has experienced the protest phase firsthand-the inescapable inner restlessness, the powerful urge to contact the person ('just to talk'), mistaken glimpses of the lost figure everywhere (a seething combination of overly vigilant scanning and blind hope). All are part of protest . . . if the separation is prolonged, a mammal enters the second stage: DESPAIR . . .Anyone who has grieved a death has known DESPAIR from the inside: the leaden inertia of the body, the global indifference to everything but the loss, the aversion to food, the urge to closet oneself away, the inability to sleep, the relentlessness of the world . . . The disease state we call major depression in human beings may be a twisted variant of the despair reaction" (Lewis et. al., 2000, p. 76-79).

Clinicians have long recognized that emotional sensations exist across all time barriers. It's not at all uncommon for a stress from childhood to impact on an adult in the here and now. He may not realize his reactions to pressure are rooted in childhood, people usually don't, but rooted in the past they are. Freud himself stated that the unconscious knows no time limitation. Painful events store in the limbic system and do become something of a "ticking time bomb", driving behavior in the present: "People rely on intelligence to solve problems, and they are naturally baffled when comprehension proves impotent to effect emotional change. To the neocortical brain, rich in the power of abstractions, understanding makes all the difference, but it doesn't count for much in the neural systems that evolved before understanding existed. Ideas bounce like so many peas off the sturdy incomprehension of the limbic and reptilian brains" (Lewis et. al., 2000, p. 118).

The limbic system filters events for us through our own past experiences. No one really sees the same event in the same way. The limbic brain will pair what it considers to be similar experiences, even though it may be mistaken: "Only a person of surpassing wisdom doubts his own mind enough to remark, as the Supreme Court Justice Robert Jackson once did when reversing himself on a point of law, 'The matter does not appear to me now as it appears to have appeared to me then.'" (Lewis et. al., 2000, p. 120).

All therapists know that we respond to others emotionally as though they were figures from our pasts. Many clients have given up on working with these very entrenched beliefs. People who have a tiny bit of faith can afford to begin anew, and trust that perhaps this new expert can help me – "them that's got shall get." Some mental health will attract greater mental health. You can get more health if you have a bit, at least enough to try anew in good faith.

The authors of <u>A General Theory on Love</u> do not feel medication can make the changes needed for a permanently higher level of comfort in the world: "For most of history, humanity has employed a handful of emotional regulators-alcohol, opium, cocaine, cannabis, a few others. All have had major drawbacks. The truly effective chemical modulation of emotionality is a dazzling scientific achievement, even if the underlying mechanisms remain impenetrable mysteries. But medications cannot resolve all limbic predicaments, not by half. What they lack in nuance they make up in strength, but sometimes nuance is called for. Early emotional experiences knit long-lasting patterns into the very fabric of the brain's neural networks. Changing that matrix calls for a different kind of medicine altogether" (Lewis et. al., 2000, p. 176).

In other words, deep belief systems must be accessed. Changing beliefs takes work: "The neocortical brain collects facts quickly. The limbic brain takes work" (Lewis et. al., 2000, p. 11).

It also takes the right kind of work. Although the practice loosely known as "talk therapy" is useful in establishing a baseline understanding of a client's history, it does not move limbic system connections. Lewis, Amini and Lannon state that it takes a new limbic system connection to revise a limbic system pattern: "Therapy worthy of the name changes what he wants. When he finishes, his heart tends in a healthier direction, the allure of the former pathology diminishes and what was once barely noticeable becomes his new longing" (Lewis et. al., 2000, p. 181).

So we see that fear and stress are virtually soldered into the brain's circuitry. PTSD is a kind of shock. It is nature's way of protecting the organism from overwhelmingly frightening experiences. It is to help the creature get through the moment. Neuroscience has found that intense fear experience doesn't go through to the thinking part of the brain first. The body may race the heart without the mind immediately being aware of why this might be happening. We find ourselves dealing with archival stimuli that have set disturbing responses in motion.

Dr. Wilhelm Reich, who studied with Freud, described how anxiety will drive out pleasure in a living organism. What he called armoring, or the tensing of the organism, created unnatural pathways in the body for the life energy. This is harmful to the person. It can create stilted responses to the world. Eventually, all of these responses become habitual. Reich felt our civilizing process itself constricted us. He said mind and body must work together for the organism/person to have health. When they work together the "bio-energy" is flowing. The person will "feel" natural to others. The energy will be high, not in a "spiked" manner, but as an even, steady flow.

Dr. Reich was creating superb affective therapies in the 1920's and 1930's. In fact, he had a very early eye movement therapy.

Dr. Reich very masterfully identified the types of neuroses commonly seen and understood how they developed and how they functioned in personality and body. He called the types of neuroses Character Types. Neurotic people lack empathy for others. As the neuroses develop further the person becomes more angry and destructive, and can even be quite sadistic (or masochistic).

We see these character types everywhere in our present culture. The lack of empathy for one another is becoming quite pronounced in American culture in 2004. We see the character types in our work, as partners in marital therapy, as parents, and in the larger society. One could argue we've learned very little about real healing and caring for each other more kindly since Reich's time. Neurotic and angry people seem to abound everywhere in our society. They are our criminals and our judges, our "drop-outs" as well as our teachers.

Reich noted the common constriction he saw in people. In every case, the maladaptive behavior was an attempt to reduce the anxiety: "The inhibition of respiration, as it is found regularly in neurotics, has, biologically speaking, the function of reducing the production of energy in the organism, and thus, of reducing the production of anxiety" (Reich, 1942, p. 276).

Reich said that anyone who does not have an energetic quality and freely moving shoulders and facial muscles is profoundly neurotic. He said all healthy people will feel a natural caring for others: "I have experienced time and again, both in myself and in many of my co-workers, that clinging to rigid barriers and laws has the function of sparing us psychic disquiet" (Reich, 1951, p. 305).

Thus, Reich said whole societies become shaped in an unhealthy way if the population is made up of untreated neurotics: "It is no accident, but supported by fact, that life-negating philosophy always emphasizes the divisive element, such as the differences among peoples in nationalism, the differences among families in family ideology, the differences of wealth in the financial principle, the differences in social rank in the authoritarian principle. On the other hand, life-asserting philosophy stresses the common element, the common biological origin of all human animals, the common features in man, animal, and nature, the common life interests and necessities, etc." (Reich, 1951, p. 95).

Thus Reich addressed the greed, nationalism, and religious and racial prejudice that seems to rise in cultures whenever fear itself rises. A mechanical neurotic cannot be anything but what he is, until successfully treated: "The mechanist cannot be anything but conservative or reactionary. He may regard his attitudes and intentions in whatever light he pleases; but the essence of his thinking is to overlook developments, to misunderstand or hate the living organism, and therefore to seek a substitute in rigid principles.

"The essence of life is to function, and therefore it is antagonistic to any rigidity. Nature knows no bureaucracy. Natural laws are functional, and not mechanistic. Even where the law of mechanistics is valid, nature abounds with variations" (Reich, 1951, p. 304).

Reich saw treatment as needing to be done one person at a time, but always addressed the society as a whole as well. He insisted all of the history and meaning of an individual's origin is in his muscular rigidity . Modern clinicians refer to these experiences frequently as "trauma" as pleasurable experiences do not lock into the body. The very "locking" is a defense by the organism against possible harm or damage. We do not do this with pleasurable experiences.

Marital and any type of family therapy will obviously be seriously impacted if one or more members of the family is very rigid and reactionary. If people have not been getting along as they have been functioning, the goal has to be change and more flexibility. Reich would say the seriously neurotic individual cannot be anything but rigid, and will not be able to succeed in family therapy without individual treatment. This is exactly what our Family-Based unit has seen again and again, thus we do separate the individuals and treat them separately for a time following our initial diagnosis of the problems.

Dr. Reich also saw in patients a longing to heal. This longing is what helps us achieve success in therapy. He explains the sadism and lack of empathy people demonstrate as a result of the frustration of this longing to heal, to be lively, to be fully alive: "Still, a deep longing for happiness in life and memory of a happy life long past, before the entrapment, has remained. But longing and memory cannot be lived in real life. Therefore, hatred of life has grown from this tightness" (Reich, 1951, p. 473).

They way in which Dr. Reich vividly described neurotic individuals has been well-documented: "In the ocular armor segment we find a contraction and immobilization of all or most muscles of the eyeball, the lids, the forehead. This is expressed in immobility of the forehead and eyelids, empty expression of the eyes or protruding eyeballs, a mask-like expression or immobility on both sides of the nose. They eyes look out from behind a rigid mask. The patient is unable to open his eyes wide, as if imitating fright. Many patients have been unable to cry for many years. In others the eyes represent a narrow slit" (Sharaf, 1983, p. 311).

Dr. Reich first identified clear physical characteristics that display the "tightness" of the neurotic. He called the physical and emotional tightness "character armoring" and then developed methods of working physically with the tightness. The patient could then experience physical and emotional relief.

Some individual treatment must be done before the person can work well with others. Defenses are automatically activated when others do not agree with us, or want to do what we want them to do. That is why we have placed such a strong emphasis on separating family members briefly for individual treatment.

All of his life Dr. Reich addressed the patriarchal, authoritarian cultures which are the cause of individual loneliness, helplessness, craving for authority, fear of responsibility, foolish mystical longing and denial, sexual misery and impotent anger and rebelliousness. He felt the pathological depression and resignation that was so widespread in the German and American culture of his day and ours to perhaps be the worst problem of all because it is so endemic.

I find Dr. Reich's observations to be as valid and fresh today as they were in his time. He described very impulsive people as people trying to "burst forth" from their armoring all at once, the result of long suppression that is no longer tolerable. He said the people we call criminals try to find the exit from the trap of neurosis, or character armoring, all at once. Their desperation is such that they don't mind colliding with their fellow beings in the process.

Many clients who cut or mutilate themselves for relief say it helps resolve pressure and shift focus elsewhere, breaking up anxiety-a kind of rush from the "trap." Dr. Reich described the goal of masochism: "To the masochist, any kind of praise represents a provocation of exhibitionistic tendencies. Wherever he stands out, he is assailed by severe anxiety. Hence, it is necessary for him to debase himself to ward off anxiety. This, naturally, is a fresh reason for feeling neglected-which provokes the whole complex of the need for love" (Reich, 1994, p. 254).

Dr. Reich had interesting things to say about client "resistance" to therapy: "A person making a trip on a poor train is hesitant to leave it as long as a new and better one is not available to take him securely to his destination. Moreover, that person begins to develop a very peculiar capacity to persevere and also begins to cherish illusions about the nature of trains" (Reich, 1994, p. 328).

He is clearly talking about the weaving of very elaborate denial systems we see everywhere in life. Dr. Reich understood that the treatment can be inherently frightening and that the client's traumatized brain fears being pried open. He cautioned therapists not be angry with patients and regard them as enemies who do not want wellness. He did not approve of the setting of arbitrary deadlines for treatment and felt many therapists lacked the requisite analytic technique to help effect healing. He cautioned against a lack of patience with the patient.

Dr. Reich understood the depth of the trauma and what it would take to help the individual improve: "I have also explained why remembering traumatic experiences is not essential for orgone therapy. It serves little purpose unless accompanied by the corresponding emotion. The emotion expressed in the movement is more than sufficient to make the patient's misfortunes comprehensible, quite apart from the fact that the remembrances emerge of themselves when the therapist works correctly. What remains puzzling is how unconscious memory functions can be dependent upon the conditions of plasmatic excitation, how memories can be preserved so to speak, in plasmatic awareness" (Reich, 1994, p. 378).

Of course, here he is talking about the mystery of how memory is so embedded in the mind AND the body. We do not know this yet in the present time.

Dr. Reich knew well what he was looking for in a healed, or healthy individual: "From a purely phenomenological standpoint, it is clear that ATTRACTIVENESS i.e., sexual appeal, can be chiefly described by the relaxed quality of a person's musculature which accompanies flowing psychic agility" (Reich, 1994, p. 328).

Dr. Alexander Lowen studied with Dr. Reich and later practiced in New York City. He worked very extensively with the body for psychotheraputic purposes and developed a number of very interesting treatment exercises for use with neurotic, "stuck" individuals.

Dr. Lowen talked about armoring and the suffering that accompanies fearing life, fearing to reach out to others, and fearing to love. He explains the causes of the blockages of the life force we see in clients:
"The awesomeness of the irrational is that is has the power to move us. It is the source of creativity and the fountain of joy. All great experiences have this irrational quality, which enables them to move us from within. As everyone knows, love and orgasm are THE IRRATIONAL EXPERIENCES WE ALL SEEK. Thus, the person who is afraid of the irrational is afraid of love and orgasm. He is also afraid to let his body go, to let his tears flow and to let his voice break. He is afraid to breathe and afraid to move. When the irrational is repressed it becomes a demonic force that may lead a sick person to destructive actions. In normal living, the irrational manifests itself by involuntary movements-the spontaneous gesture, the sudden laugh,

even the twitching of the body before one falls asleep" (Lowen, 1967, p. 211).

Dr. Lowen also explains how armoring develops. Both he and Wilhelm Reich saw it as a result of interpersonal exchanges which have frightened the organism: either discrete or contextual trauma can be a root cause. There is a kind of "shut down" in the individual to void pain or threat. "When an inhibition against some feeling must be maintained indefinitely because its expression is not accepted in the child's world, the ego surrenders its control over the forbidden action and withdraws its energy from the impulse. The holding against the impulse then becomes unconscious, and the muscle or muscles remain contracted because they lack the energy for expansion and relaxation. This energy can then be invested in other actions that are acceptable, a process which gives rise to the ego image.

"Two consequences result from this surrender. One is that the musculature from which energy is withdrawn enters into a state of chronic contraction or spasticity that makes the expression of the inhibited feeling impossible. The impulse is, thus, thus, effectively suppressed, and the person no longer feels the inhibited desire. A suppressed impulse is not lost. It lies dormant below the surface of the body where it does not affect consciousness. Under intense stress or with sufficient provocation the impulse can become so highly charged that it breaks through the inhibition or block. This happens in a hysterical outburst or a murderous rage. The second consequence is a diminution in the energy metabolism of the organism. Chronic muscular tensions prevent full natural respiration and so decrease the energy level. The person may get enough oxygen for ordinary activities, as so his basal metabolism may appear normal. However his breathing difficulty will show up in situations of stress either as an inability to get sufficient air or more likely as an inability to cope with the stress.

"Now the body condition forces the dialectic to work in reverse. The physical situation shaped the individual's thinking and self-image. He will necessarily avoid situations that can evoke his suppressed feelings. He will justify this avoidance by developing rationalizations about the nature of reality. These maneuvers are ego devices to prevent the emotional conflict from becoming conscious. For this reason they are called ego defenses. Other ego defenses are denial, projection, provoking and blame casting. These defenses are supported by the energy withdrawn from the conflict. The individual is now characterlogically armored against the suppressed impulses. On the physical level, he is guarded by chronic muscular tension. Immured as he is by this process, he can nevertheless function in a limited way or in restricted areas" (Lowen, 1975, p. 144).

Dr. Lowen explains very clearly how a character structure manifests in a life. The ways in which a person responds to fear is as varied and interesting as individuals themselves. He said the oral character does not want to reach out. The masochistic character will try and reach, but then fear drives him to withdraw. The phallic-narcissistic character will greedily grasp, a grasp that means the person is afraid of failure or loss. He said the hysterical character has an intense kind of pride that says the other cannot hurt him if the patient refuses to love at all. Dr. Lowen said what we call loving others is really a demand for love for ourselves. "I want you to love me." We see many relationships that seem to have all kinds of subtle clauses and demands of the other, much like some type of odd business agreement. Always the threat is implied, "If you break this contract, you lose me." The other individual is always hoping for an unconditional love, creating serious friction.

Because the armoring began to form in childhood, it is well-embedded. This makes very strong, targeted treatment necessary. Individuals must be approached separately as their past experiences will very, and the armoring and character issues will vary. All of the armoring makes it difficult to be a couple or a family, however. It is easy to see why many therapists would like to see very compassionate raising of children become the norm, as prevention is always the most efficacious way to health. Barring prevention, the earlier in life good treatment can begin, the better the prognosis for the person. We tend to form very deep beliefs and then note experiences in life that prove we are "right" about life. We collect them through the years. We tend to not note experiences that do not fit our hypotheses about life. Those are discarded.

Dr. Lowen felt we see a very large amount of narcissism in our culture. He said people regularly use sexual closeness to avoid true intimacy. Sex then is a mechanical act, with each partner actually relating to a fantasy partner. Greater than the danger of presenting one's body is the danger of presenting one's heart to possibly again feel disappointment in another.

He said Freud was correct in stating that we purposely avoid overstimulating the self when we are very armored. The organism, being partially "shut down" fears the environment and its highly charged energies. As stated, when the build-up of suppression becomes too great, the organism may break out of it in surprising ways.

The traumatized brain often has very self-destructive impulses: "If a person can accustom himself to the idea of catastrophe, its sting is eliminated and its terror blunted. If one has nothing to gain, there is no risk of losing anything. A punishment that is self-inflicted is intended to avert a greater punishment by outside agents. This is the explanation of the beating fantasies or the actual beatings sought by masochistic individuals, as Wilhelm Reich showed in his analysis of the masochistic character. In masochism, the actual punishment is always less than the feared punishment, which is castration. Similarly, a self-imposed isolation is less frightening than abandonment and death" (Lowen, 1967, p. 94).

Dr. Lowen said the mind cannot deal with the unknown; the vulnerability it creates is too great. It can cope with specific fears, but a person may actually suicide to avoid the unknown doom he fears.

The character armoring, or responses to trauma create many impediments to relationships. How an individual deals with his need for love and pleasure and the way he feels about human intimacy are very defined by his character armoring. The schizoid individual will try to avoid real intimacy and will create odd behavior to protect him and ward off others. The oral character will relate in a very infantile way, but he can establish some intimacy. It may not be very satisfying to the other and will not be very reciprocal in giving love. It will not be generous. A true psychopathic character will only deal with those who are dependent and need him. He must be in control; he will then allow a kind of limited intimacy. The masoschistic character is willing to be intimate. He will also be very submissive. He fears asserting any negative feeling and will be quite dishonest with the other. The rigid character will be intimate with another but beneath it all, he will always be a very guarded person, showing only what he plans to show the other.

It is easy to see how these defenses are barriers to treatment and good family relationships. It is very important for clinicians to understand that these responses to trauma are very deeply rooted and the therapy process itself will set up tremendous anxiety. It takes solid, persistent work, as both Dr. Reich and Dr. Lowen repeatedly taught. The largest cause of treatment failure, in my opinion, is that clinicians and clients do not apply effort consistently enough, with enough force of will, and long enough. If the effort is thorough, there will be a good result. Again, I believe the analogy to physical health is relevant. One can have a healthy body, and repair an ailing body, if the principles applying to the conditions are followed with consistency, force of will, and with a long enough duration of time.

Lowen discusses what it takes to genuinely heal: "The third conclusion introduces a note of humility to this discussion. We cannot change ourselves by an effort of will. That is like trying to pull one's self off the ground by one's bootstraps. The change will occur when one is ready, willing and able to change. It cannot be forced. It begins with self-acceptance and self-awareness and, or course, with a desire to change. The fear of changing, however, is momentous. My own fear of death through a heart attack is an example. One must learn patience and gain tolerance. This is a body phenomenon. The body gradually develops a tolerance for a more energetic way of life, stronger feelings and freer and fuller self-expression" (Lowen, 1975, p. 117).

Although the work can be difficult, there are many good clinicians working at this time who do understand the dynamics of healing, mentally and physically: "When the energy that is available to give life and vitality to a person does not flow, stasis results with a jamming (confusing overactivity) in the central nervous system. This jamming is manifest as 'chatter' in the mind. The musculature responds by 'holding' or blocking flow. The more internal chatter we have, the less external input our nervous apparatus is able to receive and act upon. This chatter is repetitious and habitual, as in a repeating tape loop. The same themes, attitudes, problems and solutions appear over and over again. In the face of this repetition, we seem helpless. These deeply ingrained habits of thought and feeling have been produced by repeated life experiences, often originating in our earliest years. As our strongest habits, they tend to dominate our behavior and govern our immediate responses to almost all situations. For example, if our parents kept giving us a mixed love/hate message, leaving us uncertain and insecure, then in later life our deepest interpersonal relations are sure to include this uncertainty. Not certain of being loved, we keep asking 'Do you love me? Do you love me? Do you love me?' either directly or through our actions. With our nervous apparatus continuously locked into this struggle, we are unable to perceive other, more nourishing energies, or to free ourselves of doubt" (Kurtz & Prestera, 1984, p. 19).

Other contemporary therapists like Jeffrey Maitland are looking at the body's response to emotional stress: "Look more deeply and you will discover that each displeasure brings with it a kind of tension that initially has no specific bodily location. If you do not try to flee or manipulate yourself by means of your habitual patterns of avoidance, you will realize that this tension is the beginning of your own mobilization of power for overcoming the obstacle. This tension is actually a kind of energy that you instinctively summon forth when confronting an obstacle. More fundamentally, it is actually a form of intentionality, an excitement over the imbalance of your present situation" (Maitland, 1995, p. 110).

In working with his own body, Maitland was surprised by the pervasive nature of problems in energy flow and attitude. The problems are extant in all of us, and they greatly impact family therapy: "I was amazed by the number and depth of unhealthy responses, attitudes, beliefs, and feelings that I had structured at every level of my being. I could hardly believe how thoroughly I had allowed popular culture and other people to form my self. Without realizing it I had taken on this contradictory mess of attitudes, feelings, and beliefs from all the trivial songs I listened to as a teenage, from television, from comics, from movies, from friends, from my parents and teachers, and many other sources. Even the attitudes and feelings I thought were stupid and empty were in some way still a part of me. I understood what Nietzsche meant when he said that you must take care in the fighting of dragons that you do not become one. In a very real way, you become what you hate" (Maitland, 1995, p. 17-18).

Maitland sees pervasive anxiety and fear in the body throughout his practice. He well understands the emotional effects of these fears: "Anxiety can be defined as the threat of non-being. In the experience of fear, you are afraid of a specific object, person, or situation, and you also have a kind of direction, or orientation in space sometimes toward but usually away from the object of fear. In anxiety, as Heidigger points out, there is no specific object about which you are anxious. The sense of being threatened does not seem to come from any one place or object, but is diffuse, seeming to come from everywhere. Because of the non-directionality of anxiety, it is useless to try to run away. Anxiety is more global than fear, it seems to be everywhere around you, and unlike fear, threatens the very core of your being. Psychospatially, I defined fear as not wanting to be present; anxiety defined psyschospatially is the threat of not being able to be present at all" (Maitland, 1995, p. 47).

Maitland understands the etiology of fear and anxiety/trauma, just as did Reich and Lowen: "Self-deception is rooted in conflicted human relationships that begin in our first attempts as children to understand the world of our parents. In order to develop appropriately, a child must become congruent with the spatializations of its parents. If the parents' psychospatial orientations are conflicted, then the child is in for a difficult time" (Maitland, 1995, p. 93).

When parents have treated children with anger, hostility and contempt, the developing child will be confused and frightened: "How can a developing child come into agreement with a mother or father who creates that kind of space?

"The child cannot want this as her experience. Unfortunately, she must come into agreement with this hostile space in order to realize that she cannot come into agreement with it. Therefore, to some extent she must block her agreement with it, her understanding of it. In order not to feel the terrible intensity of her parent's threatening orientation, she instinctively uses the boundaries of her developing body-self to defend herself against the hostility of this space at both a core and surface level" (Maitland, 1995, p. 93).

Again, we are talking about a powerful denial or suppression. The suppression will not disappear forever, however, and one day will surface. Dr. Arthur Janov has been doing excellent affective work for years: "'Let me be.' is the frequent scream we hear in our therapy . . . Therapy must drain that pool over time to lower the burden of pain and allow the system to right itself. This is done by reliving one bit of a feeling at a time, integrating and resolving it. It is the transformation of pain into feeling. That is how neurotics become feeling human beings" (Janov, 1991, p. 28-30).

Dr. Janov noted that even infants in particular will block and gate responses to pain, putting them in storage for a lifetime. They then will become the source of later tension throughout the life: "Hopelessness is at the bottom of so much acting out. I recall seeing one radical activist who was constantly engaged in one cause or another trying to make a better world. The feeling he had in therapy was, 'I have to make a better home life or I'm going to die.' The world he was making outside was but a substitute for the better world he needed at home . . . Symbolic acting out is probably as diverse as people. The person who has to accumulate money finally gets rich, yet needs more to keep himself from finding out that there was nothing to get. Money becomes a substitute for lack of love. Money, in fact, is a frequent substitute for love. Those who were deprived early in life often have an inordinate need for money. Some simply steal it. They want something for nothing; they want to feel loved without having to do anything for it. Stealing is a symbol of that need" (Janov, 1991, p. 132-135).

Dr. Janov is also clear in his understanding that the cognitive thinking system will not unlock neurosis: "To understand an act-out, even to understand that it is neurotic, won't change a thing. It would be the same faulty logic to imagine that understanding a virus would cure an infection" (Janov, 1991, p. 138)

Dr. Janov's comments on addiction are quite interesting: "The problem I have with this is the moralizing character of it, the insistence on self-discipline, commitment to change, etc, which the person can pay lip service to while pain rages down below. His major commitment has been to try to get comfortable; along the way he got addicted. He was committed to normalizing himself despite the opprobrium that it brought.

"I am by no means against treatment of illness. I believe that one can be helped with drug addiction or alcoholism in drying-out centers. Counseling also helps to handle day-to-day problems. One must control one's diet to reduce hypertension, and use drugs to control its fluctuations. But this is an endless task. Beating back history is not the same as resolving it" (Janov, 1991, p. 215-274).

Dr. Janov talks about the fear clients have of succeeding at love and what this fear is actually about. Of course, this has profound implications for couples' and family therapy: "Struggle is a symbolic way the neurotic goes abut getting fulfilled. The neurotic rarely goes straight for love. On the contrary, the pattern is first to find a neurotic like your parent then STRUGGLE to get love. You find a cold woman and try to make her warm. You find a critical, unsatisfied man and try to make him accepting. The struggle for love is what is ingrained, not the getting of it. Getting apparent love often makes the neurotic feel worse because the underlying feeling is of being unloved.

"Being warped early in life means that neurotic parents placed a condition on love, the condition that you be what they need instead of what you are. As long as a parent needs, that will always be true. Neurotics avoid normals. They won't be your drinking buddy, and they won't gamble alongside you. They won't flatter your ego nor build your self-esteem. You cannot use the normal to construct your own personality" (Janov, 1991, p. 308-311).

Dr. Janov defines the dilemma of love as a fear of being loved, because once before you felt that feeling and it was brutally taken away. These beliefs are deeply encoded into the traumatized brain. They are the impediment to successful relationships of all kinds.

My team recently treated a girl who had been brutally sexually abused and traumatized. She was being returned home after two bouts of residential treatment. In my opinion, the treatment had been somewhat incomplete and had not fully resolved the trauma for the girl. We did the trauma treatment and she began to calm. We then began to experience difficulty with the mother. She was inordinately fearful. It's true the girl had come home and failed once, but the mother was so anxious and overly protective of the girl it seemed to us that explanation was not reasonable. As we probed the mother's history further we discovered that when she was much younger she lost an infant son in a horrible fire. Worse, the fire was set by her alcoholic father who was babysitting the child. He burned down the house. Of course, we began treatment for her suffering. This is not the type of situation that can be handled by standard cognitive therapy. She was unable to calm in the most basic way; her limbic system regarding children and loss was far too activated. Following the affective treatment of the mother, she was able to "let up" on the girl, and began to experience that her daughter had indeed grown and was going to succeed at home at last.

The pressure of severe limbic pain for all key members of the family must be lowered or the case will not succeed. I still recall a serious clinical error we made with the "R" family. The family had five children. The father was a hard working tool and die worker. The family had a good income and a small and pleasant home. The children's mother was a volatile ethnic woman. She "led off" with an attack on us. She called the County, full of baseless, vigorous complaints almost before we even started.

Her middle son, a small overweight fellow, had fallen prey to a neighborhood pedophile. He lured the eight year old with attention, video games, and much appreciated gifts. The boy had encopresis and was very agitated and upset much of the time. The school had a hard time with him.

We treated the boy. We treated the father with good affective work and he was able to mourn some issues and strengthen, as was the boy. We did not want to treat the mother. People do not understand the degree to which treatment is a two-way street. We must also trust the client to use our best tools, tools which can be a bit unpredictable. The mother's attacks had undermined our best effort, which we had been willing to give.

We brought this family out of balance in an unfortunate way. The job was to strengthen both parents and the client. By strengthening the parents, we could then place demands upon them, chiefly that they monitor the children better. If someone is involved with their children, parents must know quite a bit about them. To not know and hope all will go well is very foolish. Our children are our most precious asset.

Because we did not trust the mother, and therefore were not able to really strengthen her, she remained working at cross- purposes with us. The boy has long since been discharged from our program, but does not look really well and happy. I vowed never again to treat family members in a vacuum. Our best work would go to all of the "key players" or none.

The family situations we have seen have been so dramatic, nothing will move the identified patient forward except affective treatment. We had the case of three brothers, who, as toddlers in their cribs, saw a stepfather murder their mother in the same room. The man then put the woman to bed, in the same room, where she remained for days. He told the boys she was ill. One of the brothers, as a latency aged child, later killed another child, and was out of the family home. I had a second brother to treat. He was in the hospital and medicated on Haldol, which is a very strong anti-psychotic medication, but still not doing well. The hospital of another company allowed me to come into their facility to begin trauma treatment. I felt we needed that safety, as I was not sure what his responses to treatment would be. He had all of the cognitions one would expect and felt sad about the death. He was also angry, and very afraid the man would one day come back and harm him, although years had passed. He did respond well to the treatment, and to this day, is living successfully in the community. Nothing but an effective trauma treatment could begin to help this boy relate to others.

References

Bradshaw, J. (1990). <u>Homecoming.</u> New York: Bantam Books.

Janov, A. (1991). <u>The New Primal Scream.</u> Wilmington, DE: Enterprise Publishing.

Kurtz, R. (1984). <u>What the Body Reveals.</u> San Francisco: Harper and Row.

Lewis, T. et. al. (2000). <u>A General Theory of Love.</u> New York: Random House.

Lowen, A. (1967). <u>The Betrayal of the Body.</u> New York: Collier Books.

Lowen, A. (1975). <u>Bioenergetics.</u> New York: Penguin Arkana.

Maitland, J. (1995). <u>Spacious Body.</u> Berkley: North Atlantic Books.

Reich, W. (1942). <u>The Function of the Orgasm.</u> New York: World Publishing.

Reich, W. (1951). <u>From Wilhelm Reich: Selected Writings.</u> New York: Farrar Straus and Giroux.

Reich, W. (1994). <u>Character Analysis.</u> New York: Farrar Straus and Giroux.

Sharaf, M. (1983). <u>Fury in the Earth.</u> New York: St. Martin's Press.

van der Kolk, B. (1987). <u>Psychological Trauma.</u> Washington, D.C.: American Psychiatric Press.

CHAPTER FOUR: THE IDENTIFIED PATIENT

Classic thinking in family therapy is that the "problem person, " the identified patient, is serving some purpose in the family. There is some problem in the level of honesty and intimacy in the family.

The identified patient may be registering a protest of some sort through his behavior. He may realize something is seriously amiss, and be attempting to call the family's attention to it. He may be sacrificing himself to protect maladaptive parents or a sibling.

John Bradshaw is a former priest who holds three degrees from the University of Toronto. He is an internationally known drug and alcohol counselor and a former alcoholic himself. He became very interested in treatment issues and has hosted three PBS television specials on treatment. He speaks very eloquently about the child, or the identified adult patient, carrying the pain for the entire family.

The child, being so vulnerable for such a long period of time, is in a bad position. He knows he needs these older, taller, "others." He doesn't know how to get food. He doesn't know how to pay the mortgage, or even that it is paid. He depends, for years, on the good will of the older people, the parents.

The child idealizes the parent. He knows he cannot risk being abandoned. Areas of sharp disagreement with the parent are rapidly moved out of consciousness. He needs to survive. He silences his true self. He may become angry and create severe developmental delays and failures by wasting time acting out the anger. The events fill up the time that he might use to contemplate what dynamics in the family disturb him. The events keep him busy so he doesn't have to confront the feared other, the older, taller one, the parent; the one with all the power.

Being a child is a very helpless position, and it is helpless for many years. Again, John Bradshaw addressed this in a very vivid manner: "The abused inmates of a concentration camp...are inwardly free to hate their persecutors. The opportunity to experience their feelings-even to share them with other inmates, prevents them from having to surrender their self...This opportunity does not exist for children. They must not hate their father, they cannot hate him...They fear losing his love as a result. Thus children, unlike concentration camp inmates, are confronted by a tormentor they love" (Bradshaw, 1990, p. 50).

European therapist Alice Miller discusses the dilemma for the child as being unable to be aware of what was done, and not having a way to tell about it. She sees patients repeating the experiences as a way of "telling" the story of what happened without offending the parent, or even bringing into consciousness that the parent was unfair.

California therapist Ron Smotherman describes the repetition of disturbing beliefs: "Sometimes we feel stuck in life. And we are stuck. What we are stuck with is a memory of an event in life which we refused to accept and therefore could not experience. Because you refuse to experience an event, it becomes stuck for you" (Smotherman, 1980, p. 61).

Again, in John Bradshaw's book, Alice Miller says: "We finally realize that all our lives we have feared and struggled to ward of something that really cannot happen any longer; it has already happened, happened at the very beginning of our lives while we were completely dependent" (Bradshaw, 1990, p. 101).

We need to look for our happiness exactly where we originally lost it: in the original family. Children want to hear one theme consistently from us: "I'm so glad I have you. It makes a wonderful difference in my life that I have you." If we are not given this feeling we will spend a lifetime trying to fill in this void. Filling the void cannot be done with material things from "without". No amount of money or number of cars will "fix" the hurtful assessments of the self given by a dad or mom. You can never get enough of what you really don't want.

Once a poor self-image is formed, no amount of praise will help us. People cannot accept honest praise or compliments. It is too cognitively dissonant. They don't believe the praiser. We will also work to create experiences that square with our beliefs and will actively filter out those experiences that seem dissonant. If I have a narcissistic wound from childhood, and believe I am not competent, I will not act competently. I will then receive feedback from the world that I am not competent, further exacerbating the wound.

There are techniques that can shift belief systems. They must be applied with great vigor and consistency to obtain the shift. Healing is an awkward path. It is not a straight trajectory, but more like an awkward game of Mother-May-I? One giant step forward is taken, but may be followed by two scissor steps sideways, and one baby step backwards. Of course, it is far simpler to build good self-esteem in childhood preventively than it is to "add it in" later in life.

The former suffering takes as many forms in the person's adulthood as there are interesting persons on the earth. One person may give up entirely, attempt to hide from life in some way. Another may become very aggressive and belligerent. Another may develop very intense fantasies and then escape into them. Escapes into addiction are very common.

We see in adulthood many who have an intense desire to control the environment and other people. Of course it causes fear and resentment in close others in the current environment, but they are attempting to never be caught in the same chaos and traps again. This guardedness takes the energy a person would ordinarily be using for attentiveness, empathy and joy in the present. We can sometimes see very aberrational behavior as the person struggles with events that transpired long ago. His significant others are often mystified by what they view as a dramatic overreaction to minor events or seemingly unimportant comments when those comments are out of context of the original trauma in the present day.

We can see interesting psychology play out in famous/infamous people in the news. Klansman/politician David Duke's sister stated that their mother was debilitated by alcohol, prescription drug abuse, and several serious strokes. Mr. Duke's response to these events is often characteristic of many children of people who are ill, in addiction. He became a perfectionist, struggling to right wrongs and make things go "right". It should be noted that his sister also described their father as strong and very demanding. Obviously, Mr. Duke also projects many of his fearful thoughts onto other groups: blacks, Jewish people, etc. It really doesn't matter who the groups are. The important thing is to project the long suppressed feelings OUT. They have been long suppressed, but still contain the high energy of the original childhood fears.

Mental health treatment is fascinating because the same etiology can produce different effects in different children. Severe scolding and emotional or physical abuse in childhood can also result in a person who is very energetic, anxious, but who makes great efforts to prove to life, to "God, " that he is good. He achieves and achieves, asking metaphorically, "Am I good? Am I good now, if I do this? Or that? When will the world say I'm good? What to do I have to do?" Others will cower from the world and not attempt anything. Some will move against others. "If you do not care for me, I will not care for you."

The challenge to the treatment person is to try to determine what has happened to the patient. Fortunately the history does not need to be ferreted out with detective-like accuracy for the treatment to be successful. More important is to determine what the person's response to events has been. What beliefs did he/she form as a result? How are those beliefs playing out in the present? And most importantly, what can I, the clinician do, to help the person change those beliefs and adapt them to needs of the present?

A human being has many long years of dependency to endure. This alone gives the child's parents a great deal of power. We see children continually deny what they are feeling to avoid difficulty with the parents. The continual disowning of the "self" to meet the "go along, get along" needs of the family begin to be a permanent part of the child's brain structures. He may even find his intellectual capacity to discern what is truly happening in the present diminish, a kind of intellectual atrophy.

Especially in the last two decades, therapists have noted the child's anxiety and his felt finitude. He borrows an armor of self-assurance from his family as best his can. In the 1930's Wilhelm Reich was working with patients and knew the treatment had to deal with the ways in which the individual's feelings of insignificance literally shaped his nerves and muscles. Much more than the intellect is affected by stressful experiences. Much more than intellect has to be incorporated into treatment.

If a parent continually overpowers or undermines a child, the surface appearance of the child may indicate the parent has "won, " or that there are no problems in the way he has handled the child. Unfortunately, there are subtle changes in a relationship in which one person has profoundly disappointed the other on a regular basis. It never feels quite "right" to the disappointed person. He may take action against the world, the parent, or himself. He WILL have some response. It may be delayed for years or be very subtle, but there will be a response. Of course we see this dynamic in marriages as well. Suddenly a person just leaves, without explanation etc.

We see dramatic traumas: sexual abuse, physical abuse, and severe emotional abuse. We also see long-term "contextual" disappointment. The child was fed, had a place to sleep, but often and over a period of years, the parent let the child down in important ways. Sometimes this results from a misguided attempt to make the child "better." Of course, spiritually, there IS nothing "better" than a child. Rev. Paul Solomon reminded parents of this obvious fact again and again. And of course, children need to be socialized and taught. But constant scolding or shaming hurts the child. He did not understand his disappointment and may not have had words for it. Or he may have understood the disappointment and been afraid to speak. A child does have an intrinsic sense of being the smaller one. He understands the "bargain": you are big. You brought me into this experience. You are supposed to support me, teach me, encourage me, be interested in me, and love me. The early impressions are amplified as he reaches school age. He sees other children, other homes, other parents. He "studies" these relationships and will make comparisons. Much of this studying may not be conscious, so it is unlikely to be verbalized.

Later in life the parent may abruptly see the child's true self. It may be released in destructive behavior. You can hear the true self with children and couples in arguing. Under the extreme stress of fighting people tend to become gruesomely honest. Things the person has long been afraid to express to the more powerful "other" will suddenly be expressed. We see a "surge" in personal power at adolescence. The adolescent may become more willing to challenge the more powerful other, the parent. In couples, what appears to be a breakdown of the relationship may actually be an increase in feelings of power by partners who have tired of the "good behavior" performed in courtship. People simply cannot keep up the extensive play-acting forever.

Being shamed and scolded, or worse, physically or sexually abused in childhood will "skew" the developing human in many important ways. The long period of human dependency during development exacerbates the vulnerability. Wise parents will shield their offspring from worldly dangers. They will even hide them from the child. What good is it for the child to know about dangers about which he can do nothing? It only serves to heighten fear and anxiety.

In explaining childhood situations to clients I sometimes use the analogy of "nicks and cuts". It's not that an artery was cut in many cases, but the many disappointments in childhood become like a series of "nicks and cuts" all over the person. There is still blood loss and a weakening of the organism. It can be cumulative, resulting in a weakened, over-reactive adult.

Sometimes the Identified Patient has experienced an abrupt, discrete trauma. Sometimes the family is unaware of this for many years, or even forever. I recall a case in which a teenaged girl, from a very nice family, suddenly began acting out and was very angry and tyrannical at home. The family knew of no reason. Several years later the girl told her parents she had been sexually molested at a swimming pool in their wealthy neighborhood. She was raped and humiliated by a group of males. She had been too ashamed and upset to let anyone know this had happened. This abuse took place over a period of only fifteen minutes at a community pool. It had then "plagued" her for years. She made a valiant effort to protect her parents from this horrible news and to deal with aftereffects of the abuse on her own. She thought others would not notice her changes in affect and behavior, but her parents were stunned and perplexed by her changes in behavior.

In therapy, in as much "safety" as possible, we need to identify unhealthy beliefs and secrets. What may have been the best operant belief a person can "muster" in childhood may now be completely dysfunctional. We need to help the client figure out what he is feeling. We need to help him figure out what he would like to happen. How can we (client, therapist, client and family) facilitate it happening?

One of the many blockages clients have a great deal of trouble with is almost a feeling of chagrin. There is an embarrassment because we have lived for a long period of time in a certain way. Once the client has gained a deep understanding, he feels foolish. He feels he should have known this (or actually did know it) for a long time. It is worth reminding the client he should make the change; he will feel even more foolish if allows more time to pass without making the change. It also becomes more difficult to make the change.

We know intrinsically what we do need. We all have a sense that we deserve a better reality. However, false beliefs that do not support life are what holds everyone back. We fear we must know pain in order to know joy. This is foolish. You don't need to listen to harsh dissonant music to know that Mozart's music is lovely. We fear we will "get in trouble" for our anger, so we move it down and experience it as depression. What we really need are negotiation skills so that those close to us will listen to our needs. Sadly, if those loved ones are too ill to listen, we may need to help them or even get different loved ones.

People greatly fear loneliness. The anxiety about keeping health, gaining money, gaining power, is anxiety about loneliness. Clients need to squarely face the fear and understand how universal it is. We can endure loneliness, even extensive loneliness. We probably won't actually need to, as good relationships are possible. It does seem like a harsh universe and it is universal in the mammal kingdom that we want companionship. The fear of loneliness is another fear that we allow to inordinately frighten us, however. This fear is always at play with the Identified Patient and his loved ones.

John Bradshaw claims that even the brilliant and able Albert Einstein uttered as his last words: "Is the Universe safe?"

We are always talking about degrees of aberrational behavior. Our identified patients are not different from the rest of us. It is a matter of degrees of maladjustment and sometimes it can even seem comical.

People can become very "locked" into cognitions that are life-destroying, yet defend them to the end. A man came in to me for treatment for severe anxiety and stress. He did seem very anxious and had trouble sitting still for the interview. He was about thirty-five years of age and had moved to Pennsylvania from New York City's west side a few years before. He unfolded a very odd story. He had been involved in organized crime since he was a teenager. Now, in Bethlehem, Pennsylvania, he was involved in a dispute with some criminals back in New York. He had the job of taking trailers of goods. He mentioned Ralph Lauren suits, and selling them in our more rural area. He owed some of the people in New York a substantial amount of money and did not have it. Nor did he any longer have the suits. He told me he was on medication, but still very nervous.

I looked at him and said, "You should be nervous."

In our next interview, he told me he wanted a change of lifestyle, soI decided to explore possible job training and work options with him. He was able-bodied and still relatively young. He had not completed high school.

When I mentioned work to him he gave me a very long, very blank stare. The silence continued. I repeated myself. We should begin to explore some work options. More silence.

Finally, he said to me quite indignantly, "WORK. I've never worked a day in my life." He huffed out of my office and never came back. He was a good example of a man holding a very dysfunctional old entitlement belief – "I don't have to work. The world owes me." Yet his beliefs have now put his life at risk. Still, he won't consider changing them. Remember, we are always talking about degrees of aberrational thought. A great many of us have variations of this kind of entitlement.

The Identified Patient is expressing needs we all have, expressing them in a successful or an unsuccessful manner. We all need to feel our lives have some importance. We want to feel our lives have made a difference in the world. It matters that we have lived. We all need the love of a least a few others. John Bradshaw says that in addition, we all need to feel our parents are "O.K."

In mental health, we are talking about degrees of complaint about the person's adjustment to the world, and his concomitant behavior. We all have some complaints, and we all act on them inappropriately at times. We're talking about degrees.

The Huge Role of Discouragement

Many clients are very problematic for the clinician. They are already so discouraged by life they see no value in attempting to better their condition.

Younger clients can be moved more easily. They have not built the years of "proof" the world is as they say it is. They have not increased their cognitions about how the world is into a massive, "cement" block.

We took a client from years of placements in residential facilities. He was very "hangdog" and delighted in annoying his parents once home. He failed at everything he touched. As we dealt with his history it became clear that the parents had very deep wounds and could not tolerate the energy of the little pre-schooler our client once had been. They convinced the mental health system to place the boy in residential facilities. He remained in them for eight years, truly falling through the cracks in case management.

We saw a basically nice, but very discouraged and resentful boy, not the dangerous borderline, anti-social personality he had been diagnosed as being. He was avoidant, and hid in fantasies about rock stars and videos whenever anything threatening was raised. We gently called him back into reality, quietly, but again and again. We corrected, again and again, the constant shaming the parents indulged in. Verbal messages from the parents were withering. As the parents backed away from their mistreatment of the boy (and they were by no means convinced that we were correct) he slowly began to calm. One of my staff members moved the case one hundred and eighty degrees on a Friday night by taking the boy to hear a mediocre, but well-known band in our area. He had seldom ever been out of his darkened home, much less to a live concert. Incidentally, good family-based programs keep contingency funds to do exactly this type of thing.

This seventeen-year-old completely came to life. He had something to live for: live concerts. He was now much easier to motivate.

He found a simple kitchen job in a restaurant in his neighborhood. The workers on the job became a kind of surrogate family for the boy, replacing the camaraderie he had never gotten from the family. He had a place he fit in. As we closed his case, the boy was on his way to his last year of high school and he fully intends to finish school and have a good life.

Pressuring these discouraged people is a difficult task: not enough pressure and the inertia rules; too much pressure, and the client disintegrates, and the clinician is left holding a "wet Kleenex." If the pressure is not balanced the clinician will find clients avoiding appointments.

Islamic teacher Sheikh Jarrar said a human being should live between two poles-hope and fear. Sheik Jarrar suggests not making a test too easy. The student will not respect it and will not prepare. If it is too difficult, he loses hope and moves into despair.

We must do our counseling between these two poles. Something must be a stake for our clients, yet the test must not be so daunting the person gives up. Often I've told my staff if we attack a person too rigorously (even for very heinous behavior) he will simply wilt on us. We'll be left holding a handful of wet Kleenex. A careful balance must be struck to maintain challenge with hope of success.

A guiding principle of psychology is that the greatest stresses involve:

A lack of predictability

A lack of way to express anger and frustration and

A lack of control.

It is easy to see how the experience of being a child creates these conditions due to the dependence and vulnerability of the human child. The child is in a bad position. Parents "push" their children to disown their feelings; we call it social training. When a child is legitimately angry at his sister her cannot hate her, not possibly. For heaven's sake, that's his sister. The child learns he must swallow his feeling again, and again. He's trying to buy peace so he can grow up.

The discouraged client takes a great deal of patience. As I tell my staff, the person is so tired of never getting a hit, and being jeered at, he won't even step up to the plate anymore.

California psychologist Nathaniel Branden has done very good work with the development of self-esteem: "The base and motor of poor self-esteem is not confidence but fear. Not to live, but to escape the terror of life, is the fundamental goal. Not creativity, but safety, is the ruling desire. And what is sought from others is not the chance to experience real contact, but an escape from moral values, a promise to be forgiven, to be accepted, on some level to be taken care of.

"Persevering is the attempt to understand in spite of difficulties. In my pursuit of understanding and mastery I sometimes encounter difficulties. When this happens, I have a choice: to persevere or give up. Students face this alternative in their school studies. Scientists fact it in struggling with research problems. Executives face it in the thousand challenges of everyday business. Everyone faces it in personal relationships.

"If we persevere in the will to efficacy yet seem stopped by a barrier we cannot move through, we may take a rest or try a new approach, but we do not surrender to despair or resign ourselves to defeat. In contrast, if we give up, withdraw, fall into passivity, or go through the motions of trying without meaning it, we shrink the level of our consciousness-to escape the pain and frustration that accompanied our efforts. The world belongs to those who persevere" (Branden, 1994, p. 76).

I agree with Branden that for the development of character and self-esteem, people must work through periods of discouragement and frustration. Our culture offers many escapes and we have developed a national philosophy that we must never feel pain. Yet the reality is that working through pain and winning out over challenges offers a sense of self that cannot be replicated any other way. Good therapists will make demands on children and adults alike. Unfortunately, the challenges of life do not get any easier, nor does the experience of moving through them become easier at thirty than it is at twenty. Clients should be kindly pushed to develop competence at all times. We're not doing a client any favor if he "loves us", feels very supported by us, but remains somewhat "infantilized." Once without the therapist, he is somewhat lost. Clients "loving us" is more about

46

the needs of the therapist. I tell my staff we are more like coaches and technicians, there to do a job, than we are dear friends. It is friendly to do the job very well and thoroughly for the client.

Many times the Identified Patient feels the world is judging him far more harshly than it is. It is an old axiom that when we are nervous about facing others we should always remember they are nervous too, and are worrying about what we think of them as much as we are worrying what they think of us. Some studies have even indicated that part of the reason we do such a poor job of listening to each other is that, in our anxiety, we are busy planning our next statements. We are too busy planning our "defense" to listen: "There is an old story about this: A rabbi is standing in front of his congregation and says, I was such a good rabbi; now I am nothing. I'm really nothing.' And so the cantor, the singer, picks it up. He says, 'God, I was such a good cantor and I am nothing. I'm really nothing.' A little tailor in the congregation picks it up. 'God, I was such a good tailor and I am nothing, really nothing. And the rabbi says to the singer, 'Who does he think he is to think he's nothing?" (Perls, 1969, p. 230).

The discouraged person presents other challenges to a treatment person. It is quite common that a person has a "chip on his shoulder". He has an attitude: I have had it so bad, I deserve this (negative self indulgence, addiction, to treat you badly, to be considered first, etc.)

Clearly, if all members of a family harbor this feeling (and we see this often), it's going to be an unsupportive internal environment for all of its members. They are virtually pushing each other down to step over that back of the other. They must get their own needs met at all costs. Thus, a place that should be a nurturing respite from the world (the home) feels like a dog-eat-dog modern corporate business instead.

Again, because of these deep core beliefs, which people are unwilling to admit, it is vital in all couples therapy and family therapy to strengthen the individual before treatment can succeed. We need to strengthen the willingness to be "real, " to expose the innermost self. Only then can we even try for family intimacy.

The Discouraged Client

Transference Issues

If a client is very rude to a therapist it is reasonable and proper to hold that client to a standard of human decency. A therapist is sot some type of servant, not someone to be acted out upon aggressively. We do not do a client a favor to allow him to continuously display and empower his most negative aspects. Behavior used frequently increases. Bad behavior leads to more bad behavior.

I challenged a teenaged girl and her mother. My staff and I had worked with this family for several years. The girl had been badly sexually abused and had had her life threatened by her natural father. She had been concomitantly traumatized and was very angry. We brought her into a good stability and moved her into a regular education placement.

A meeting was held with the county to review and continue services. I had informed the client I was not able to attend that meeting as I had to be with another client. I was later told she had complained about my work and generally criticized my every effort, but she still wanted my services as a therapist. At our next session I confronted the girl and her mother. It told them I thought we had a reasonable working relationship and I was very hurt and angry by this disloyalty. I did not expect to do my best work and then be "snake bitten" by her the moment my back was turned. This teenager had recently been confronted by an angry peer for the very same behavior and I reminded her of this fact. This type of situational loyalty is a behavior that does not work in life.

I was serving this girl well to let her feel my disapproval, allow her to "own" and understand this offending behavior, and heal the relationship. In a safe environment (in predictable therapeutic sessions) I showed her forgiveness and continued to work with her in

48

a normal manner. Following a confrontation in her peer group, complete avoidance would have been the experience. No growth would have been the experience.

Mandated Therapy

I do not feel mandated therapy needs to necessarily be an obstacle. The same principle of "wooing" the client applies. We all do want a successful, fulfilling life. Keeping that in mind, it's quite "ok" to press and press the mandated clients.

About a third of them will ultimately respond and be very appreciative that the clinician had the courage and energy to "push" them.

When interfacing with any of the government systems and doing mandated therapy, a very deep level of honesty is very important. There is so much dissembling and outright dishonesty in many of these systems, the client must be able to believe his therapist is honest with him. Even when the news is bad, we tell a client the absolute truth. If we need to report a client's behavior to the justice system or to a youth services system, we talk to them and advise them this is what we now find necessary before anything is done. We give them our reasons if they are not immediately clear. I have not found many clients unable to handle this. They usually have an understanding of our position. They may not like what is coming, but we have been able to keep a therapeutic relationship intact much more often than might be expected.

Transference and the Sex of the Therapist

I have found this to be largely irrelevant. I know it's supposed to be relevant, but it isn't. My present treatment unit consists of three males. They are very skillful. They are able to treat the most damaged male or female sex abuse sufferer. Obviously, they are highly skilled in the use of affective treatment.

I am a middle-aged woman. I am quite able to be a "hero" or model for a fourteen-year-old boy. It's a matter of having a therapist with a "good solid core" as one of my workers phrases it. The person needs to have a very strong locus of control. If the therapist feels solid and personally empowered to the client, he will accept her as a good model for him. It's very important for the therapist not to display fear or uncertainty. The therapist is s leader, much as a general is a leader. "This is how we are going to fight this fight…" Testing of the treatment person will occur, but it will with male therapists as well.

Kids want to know you have something worth sharing. Why else would they want to listen to you? Why would they want to be like you?

Quite often kids don't respect us. They don't respect any adults. They live in a very unpleasant environment. It's all they've ever known. They don't think we can be effective. (Sometimes we can't.) They've never seen any adult be effective. This can also be true of adult clients as well, of course. Many adults have been through ineffective therapy and have made a quiet decision they must be so ill, so damaged, that they cannot be helped. They are very reluctant to try anything again. They may be ashamed to admit this to a new clinician.

<u>Interfacing with the Public Systems</u>

We get a large number of public cases that are really abuse cases. The overburdened Children and Youth and Juvenile Probation systems cannot afford to place another individual, and the local agency is hoping against hope we can be effective with a family. Agencies are financially strapped and often do not fulfill their public mandate. In the worst scenarios, a child remains in a very abusive or neglectful situation day after day and counselors are expected to go in and "pat his hand". We need to be active advocates for children and sometimes force government to move. What must children think of adults when counselors stand by helplessly or are indifferent to their plight? What must they think of the world and its indifference?

If we cannot alter the environment enough to really stop the abuse, and the agency won't place the child with relatives or in foster care, I will close the case. To continue and be ineffective says to the child we don't care what is happening to you, and even if we did care, we're ineffective in the face of the aggressive force attacking you. I almost have a visual image of us patting a child's hand lovingly while someone nearby beats him bloody. It's not acceptable. What a horrible message. Better to simply be beaten.

Use a Sense of Humor

A therapist should always demand respect. I never allow a client to speak to me too rudely. I will leave in the moment and try again in the following session with the client. It serves no value whatsoever to allow the client to verbally jab at the clinician. I have seen treatment people try and pretend the jabbing is not happening. That tells the person we are both in denial, not honest, AND cowardly. Yet we are asking this person to model himself after us.

It's important to gently confront the rudeness. I see nothing wrong in telling the client I too, have feelings, and would prefer to be treated in a kinder manner. Being treated rudely is not going to destroy me, but I am not paid to take extreme abuse, nor does it serve any value. So I tell rude clients, therefore, today, I am going to end this session. I will make a joke, if I can think that rapidly, and leave the situation.

Whenever possible, I like to couch all messages in humor. It often helps me get through an embarrassing situation. A sense of humor is so vital. I have always admonished my staff to never ever laugh at a client or show disrespect. Clients have sometimes made this very difficult. We ourselves can be quite ridiculous and comical at times.

I secured permission from our company to pay for a room at the local diner in which we could safely meet one family. Our client's mother, quite short and very overweight, had enormous breasts. She was dressed in a tight velvet leisure suit. She was not comfortable in the booth, and, to the high amusement of the two male therapists, she pulled her enormous breasts up and flopped them out onto the table, throwing the silverware asunder. The meeting to clarify issues was nearly destroyed when she said, "All right, let's just put it all out on the table."

The return of empathy can indicate healing in an individual. I vividly recall a heavy boy I began work with when he was twelve years of age. He was very violent and agitated and often needed restraint in school. He was grossly overweight and ate very obsessively. The first walk I ever took with him, in a tough part of Allentown, was quite a thrill. He called in to the angry adults who were washing their clothes in the laundromat: "Why don't you wash your mouth out while you're at it?" causing a gentlemen to wave his closed fists at us. I glanced away for a moment as we reached his doorway, feeling relieved. "C" picked up several stones and fired them as hard as he could across the street at a man who was feeding a parking meter.

"C" had been held at gunpoint as a toddler and sexually abused by his mother's paramour. For one thing, I have to wonder what kind of a man needs a gun to coerce a toddler…This happened to the boy repeatedly as the man lived with his mother. The mother told me that "C" would sit at the door and sob hysterically whenever his mother left the home. "C" endured the abuse for at least two years. He did not speak of it until many years later. Of course the threats on his life cause more "firing" of stress chemicals than the initial sex abuse. It left "C" a very ill and frightened boy. Genetically, the chief job of the mind is to keep the body alive. What very frightening repeated experiences for a small boy.

After two years of careful, TINY, doses of affective treatment (it was all "C" would allow, his fear level was so high) finally, one magical day, he offered me one of his corn chips. He had never before offered to share anything at all. Yes, we're on our way I thought. The return of empathy.

People with such severe abuse and losses are busy tending their own pain. They have too much static in front of their eyes to even briefly regard what someone else may need.

Empathy occurs naturally in the healthy. The beginnings of the return of empathy are the beginnings of healing. The person, at least momentarily, feels secure enough to risk moving the focus onto another. In this case, a boy with a severe eating disorder who ate very greedily, was finally willing to risk giving away a corn chip.

Cruelty to animals is always a very large and serious indicator of lack of empathy and is regarded as a very important symptom. It's bad enough when we see cruelty to animals in a child, but far worse when we see it in a parent. It should always be a cause for concern when and individual is willing to harm a helpless animal. We treated a very cute young boy of four who had ritualistically lined up hamsters and killed them. He had artistic talent and was quite articulate. As the case progressed, we learned his father had tried to drown him in a bathtub following an argument with his wife. He was much too small to act against this overpowering adult. But as Dr. Wilhelm Reich had stated, the anger and fear never really just disappears. What is does do is take another form, until treatment helps calm the person.

Dr. Arthur Janov has made many interesting observations about the child entering into a life. He feels strongly that when a child is not put with its mother immediately, he is imprinted with a terror and a horrible feeling of aloneness. He said children who presently need the light on in order to sleep are telling us they don't feel safe. Following the dark transition of birth, it was the light that offered respite-the light and the fact that the warm, familiar mother was there. All of Dr. Janov's many excellent books talk about the angry child-he sees him much later, as an adult. The cries again and again are that the parent stopped the child's expression of himself.

We must always remember the Discouraged Client is discouraged for a reason. It is up to us to accurately ferret out the history, help the client understand what decisions he made about the history, as try to "coach" him into more functional, life-affirming decisions. Some wise clinicians are now asking, instead of what's wrong with this person, what has happened to this person?

There is no doubt the client has experienced a great deal of shame in his early years. We feel shame whenever our interest or joy is impeded by some force. There is an element of upset over the public perception of our failure to meet the desire. Original families that are not supportive expose a child to shame over and over in these ways.

References

Bradshaw, J. (1990). <u>Homecoming.</u> New York: Bantam Books.

Branden, N. (1994). <u>Six Pillars of Self-Esteem.</u> New York: Bantam Books.

Perls, F. (1969). <u>Gestalt Therapy Verbatim.</u> Moab, Utah: Real People Press.

Smotherman, R. (1980). <u>Winning Through Enlightenment.</u> San Francisco: Context Publications.

CHAPTER FIVE: THE PARENT

How We Develop Narcissistic Needs

Parents fail their children in the ways they themselves were failed. We can't give another that we have never possessed ourselves. The health of the parent, or the individual marriage, is obviously going to be key in effecting a healthy unit. Each person must be able to function in a reasonable, autonomous manner. The issue is genuine emotional health, not "communication." I don't know how many times I have seen "good communication" listed as a need on a treatment plan. In one way I regard it as a joke. People are always communicating. When we say they're not, it usually means the communication is being withheld. The other has decided the person is not worth communication with, or not safe to communicate with. The "withhold" itself is a communication. Sometimes "no communication" or the request for improved communication means that the recipient doesn't like what's being communicated. He doesn't like what is being received and wants the therapist to magically coerce a different communication from the other.

We've been called in to many situations in which a child is at serious risk of a failed life, but find a parent who is only interested in telling us what he/she is going through. Lifelong patterns of relating to others are formed very early in our lives. Remediating these patterns later in life is far more difficult than creating supportive patterns that soothe the limbic system early in the child's life. The corny old expression is true for both physical and mental health. An ounce of prevention really is worth more than a pound of cure.

Object Relations Theory tells us that an infant is in a good world. He doesn't know he is not the center of the universe. He learns gradually he must wait and that other people have needs which may impede his own. He begins to mature and understands, through a number of humbling experiences, the myriad of things he cannot do and doesn't know. Being a small child is a very vulnerable experience.

Problems in the way parents "mirror" his value and what he is can impact a child for all of his life. The parents' own unmet narcissistic needs are usually the cause of the difficulty. They cannot give what they themselves lack.

Dr. Heinz Kohut taught us important lessons in Object Relations. The child learns who he is from the feedback from the parents. As we are developing, we know a "cup" is a cup because the parent told us so. That's how we know what an elephant is. A zebra. The parents seem to be all wise, all powerful. The most important thing we teach our children is the Einstein question. Is the Universe safe? Or at least navigable?

I can recall my daughter as a small girl with a bad cold. She insisted I could cure her fever right then and there if only I wanted to. She really believed this. I was just being mean, not doing it. I was that powerful to her.

Emotions begin in children as young as six months of age. Newer thinking says they are present in the infant at birth, perhaps even before. A six month old can show wariness. At seven months a child can clearly show joy. At nine or ten months a baby can recognize people. Some mothers will say this occurs earlier. Children as young as eighteen months of age have displayed clear signs of anxiety.

A "mixed" attachment is the most problematical attachment for a child to deal with. Sometimes the parent responds well and cares for the baby, sometimes he/she does not. This confusion is very painful for a child. The continued disappointment breeds serious resentment. It is a precursor to Borderline Personality Disorder and Narcissistic Disorders. It may be the more painful because a child does see what is possible with a caregiver. The caregiver could be "good" all the time.

Self-esteem is the appropriate sense of regard for the self. It is formed over years in development. It is part of the declarative memory. It is our interpretation of all of the things that have happened to us over the years and what they meant about our value. It is a cognitive concept. Is the Universe safe?

It is difficult for a child to feel important and valued, say, if his Dad never called. It is difficult for a child to feel important if his Mom repeatedly let her children know how much parenting had strained her resources. It is not going to be possible for a therapist to "paste" self-esteem onto a child and expect him to ignore his declarative memory which has stored many negative experiences.

Because of large numbers of activist foster parents and adoptive parents who struggle with their children, there is a growing focus on attachment problems. These committed people have been very determined and dedicated in attempts to find solutions to the mental health problems of their children. They have been creative and it has often paid off. People are seeing that early neglect cannot be made up easily, and however well intended we are, a secure attachment to others cannot be easily "pasted on" to a child: "'Without someone specifically oriented to his needs', wrote the psychoanalyst D.W. Winnicott, whose work helped inform attachment theory, 'the infant cannot find a working relation to external reality. Without someone to give satisfactory instinctual gratifications, the infant cannot find his body, nor can he develop an integrated personality. Without one person to love and to hate, he cannot come to know that it is the same person he loves and hates, and so cannot find his sense of guilt, and his desire to repair and restore." Without what the prominent psychologist Mary Ainsworth called a 'secure base' – a reliably loving person to whom a toddler can return periodically for emotional refueling-he will not feel free to explore. Relaxing into his dependency is, paradoxically, the first step to independence. Although attachment theorists generally assume that the person with whom a baby is figuring all this out is her mother, nothing in the theory excludes a loving father from filling the same role.

"Ainsworth now had a flash association: 'The behavior of these avoidant one-year-olds, I realized, was similar to the older child who has had a long depriving separation and comes home and ignores mother. Here were these kids who had never had a serious separation behaving just that way. The avoidant response suggested not only that both the infant and the older child had experienced a similar sense of rejection, but that they were using the same defense to cope with it when placed in a situation of heightened stress-an emotional cutoff that disguised their hurt and anger, even from themselves. Ambivalent children, in contrast, although angry, had not crossed over into this protective state of indifference. They still hoped for solace and connection, but their anger spoiled the possibility of getting it" (Talbot, 1998, p. 27).

How often do we seen children and teenagers, even adults acting in just this manner? I want the solace and connection, but I am angry at you for not giving it before, so I'm not going to show you I want it. You should have already read my mind and freely given it. If I have to ask, its value is diminished. The self-isolating behavior further alienates the very desired loved one. Of course, we see this dynamic in marital therapy frequently: "The behavior of the insecurely attached child…often tries the patience of peers and adults alike. It elicits reactions that repeatedly reconfirm the child's distorted view of the world. People will never love me; they treat me like an irritation; they don't trust me; or, I always feel that I need them more than they need me.

"The anxious child must inevitably feel that there is something wrong with him and something wrong with the immense love that flows out of him toward his parents and is somehow not accepted.

"Clinical evidence suggests that parents cannot tolerate seeing their unmet needs expressed by their children, and they cannot tolerate the anger and distress the child expresses when those needs go unmet again. They either overreact or become dismissive, with the result that the child's attachment feelings-as well as his anger and distress are either walled off from his consciousness or revved up to the point where they overwhelm him. His ability to communicate his attachment-related feelings is gradually shrunken and distorted until it demands misinterpretation. This fairly well describes the avoidant condition, further complicated by shame" (Karen, 1994, p. 231-247).

As stated, if the feedback to the infant is not warm and interested, difficulties begin with the baby: "Kohut viewed development in terms of the self forming in a relationship, neither in isolation nor from drives. A infant is born into a human environment. The child does not yet have a self, but the parents act and respond to the child as if it already had a self. The child sense of self arises as a result of the relationship-that is, the interplay between the infant's innate potentials and the responsiveness of the adult selves or self objects. It is not totally unlike the intake of foreign particles to build your own proteins" (St. Clair, 2000, p. 142).

When this mirroring does not go well, narcissistic disorders can appear: "Freud (1914-1957) compared narcissism to a sleeping or ill person who withdraws all emotional investment from external things, with the result that such a person is indifferent to all that is outside herself, because all the energy and attention is focused on the self" (St. Clair, 2000, p. 140).

Dr. Kohut saw the heuristic effects of the poor mirroring in this way: "If we make efforts on behalf of someone who is indifferent and non-responsive to us, we feel helpless and empty, with a lowered self-esteem and a narcissistic rage.

Narcissism, then, continues throughout life, being transformed into various forms. Healthy narcissism is manifested in adulthood in such forms as creativity, humor, and empathy" (St. Clair, 2000, p. 146).

Dr. Kohut said that it is not so much what parents do, but what they ARE that will shape the child's character. If the parents are at peace with themselves, and have the ego strength to shine where they realistically may, the child will be able to do the same. The developing child needs to be able to return to the parents, their offer of tranquility, their self-confidence, their smiles of encouragement. If they can do this, he will be very able to withstand the blows to his grandiosity that the harsh world inflicts. He will heal, and go forth into the world again. Kohut also feels that if the parents are able to consistently display their ideals and weather their disappointments bravely, the child will also have ideals. Even the mere closeness of the parent's relaxed body will long sustain the developing child. The early "safe harbor" that the parents can provide the child will serve him all of his life in his future.

Dr., Kohut speaks of the often seen problem of a parent who has an insecurely established self. This parent will respond to his OWN needs, and not those of the developing child.

Poorly mirrored children will exhibit compulsive behaviors such as headbanging if toddlers, excessive masturbation and daredevil activities if older. Lonely "unmirrored" adults will seek excitement in compulsive ways in sexual and non-sexual arenas. The person may be hypersocial and prone to drug and alcohol and other addiction problems. The joy of the total self is unavailable to the person because of the poor early mirroring, thus he seeks sensations in the present in an effort to break out of his contextual depression.

Dr. Heinz Kohut identified two types of problematic transference that result in narcissistic personality disorders. The mirror-transference is one in which the source of accepting-confirming did not adequately do this for the developing person. The idealizing transference is one in which an idealized source of strength and calmness does not present for the developing individual to merge with. These early losses result in a weakened or defective sense of self.

Dr. Kohut indicated this weakened self is less able to weather swings in self esteem related to life's inevitable victories and defeats. Vitality will easily become depleted and the person is subject to empty depressions.

He identified the twentieth century's "understimulated self" who has suffered a prolonged lack of stimulation as a child. The young personality will lack vitality and will be experienced as boring and apathetic. He may head-bang as a child, using what few resources he has to stimulate the self. Later development may evince such activities as compulsive masturbation and daredevil feats or addictions. The total self feels joy is prohibitive, and the lonely, "un-mirrored child" will seek pleasure wherever he can.

The "overburdened self" is one in which the child did not have the opportunity to merge with a calm self-object. This child will grow up experiencing the world as very hostile and dangerous because he never learned to self-soothe. The early self-object was not empathetic and did not have such skills himself/herself.

Un-mirrored children were used to brace up the precariously constituted parent. The child's needs were never considered.

A narcissistic adult may suddenly burst into rages that seem to have no etiology; the "child" is demanding that the wrong that was done be immediately set right. Grandiosity and senses of entitlement can lead un-mirrored adults into some very unfortunate behavior and certainly make these individuals difficult for close others to accept and deal with.

People may become "merger hungry" (co-dependent) and demand the continuous presence of the significant other to bolster the new precariously constituted self. Contact-shunning personalities, paradoxically, recognize the enormous need for the other as far too intense and realize they have a great sensitivity to rejections. They may also fear being swallowed up and thus destroyed by the needed other. These persons are quite aware the self is precariously constituted and real union with another carries risk of "annihilation."

The Parent

Narcissistic clients and parents are deeply ashamed and may be uproariously difficult and assertive to guard vulnerability and keep the therapist off balance. The patient must kindly be guided to his helplessness as the "unmirrored child" and be taught to identify and meet his own needs as an adult. The client will fear rebuff and personal disintegration throughout this process and the therapist must remain gentle and firm.

Narcissistic persons, with their desire to be "looked at" are vulnerable indeed. All failures in their pursuits of perfection and success will be met with shame and rage. The "defective selves" fear, in attempting to meet their needs they will be re-exposed to the terrible mortifications they suffered as young children. Even a suicide seems a remedial act, avoiding mortification.

The "punishment" for shame is abandonment and rejection. All of the parents and all of the Identified Patients have these fears at play in one form or another. They are universal. We all have them; again, it's a matter of degree.

A psychological context of "shame-anxiety" may appear. This is referred to in this book as contextual trauma; the trauma is not isolated, or discrete, but has become part of the "fabric" of the family over a period of years. When we "transgress" we may feel guilt because we voluntarily made a negative choice. The stimulus to shame is more involuntary; we fear deficiency. A general shame-anxiety begins to permeate the life. All efforts to improve the life are truncated. The adults won't try for an education, a better job, a kinder mate. The children won't try in school, in sports, with peers. Shame must be experienced in proximity to a "perceiving other". By the time the anxiety is generalized, however, it can be ANY others. The person is left with a great many unsafe environments. All of us have seen this dynamic play out with people who become afraid to leave a safe, small little environment, usually the home.

Any time the individual moves to meet an ideal goal, and fails to do so, he is at risk of new mortifications: the "public" failure, and the secondary rejection or abandonment by others due to the failure all have been "seen" publicly. As I have stated, it has been my experience that others are very worried about their own failures and are less focused on ours than patients generally think, but this takes some convincing for the frightened client. Repeated shaming will depress a person. He will stay depressed until cognitions change.

Elie Weisel talked poignantly of his shame as a teenager in a World War II concentration camp. He felt the "burn" of the human condition very acutely and was quite upset that he did not come up to his own standards of brave behavior: "It was daytime when I awoke. And then I remembered that I had a father. Since the alert, I had followed the crowd without troubling about him. I had known that he was at the end, on the brink of death, and yet I had abandoned him. I went to look for him. But at the same moment this thought came into my mind: 'Don't let me find him. If only I could get rid of this dead weight, so that I could use all my strength to struggle for my own survival, and only worry about myself.'" (Weisel, 1985, p. 111).

There is a social aspect to shame. We have been seen to fall short, either in morality, or in some way were seen to desire something or to be something and not able to achieve this. And we were seen in a public way.

Anthropologist Charles Darwin, in his many studies, noted that we do not see children under two years of age blush. Some others have said they have noted a kind of shame-based moving away from a desire that might mean the child is experiencing shame. Certainly we do know that even young babies can develop simple goals.

Ordinary social activity can create a shaming experience in a number of ways. Some examples are:
Clearly inappropriate behavior, like exposed nakedness.
A perceived failure: at work, in public, in a relationship, can be shaming.
Incompetent social behavior that is clearly awkward and lower-class.
Attracting too much notice in public, especially with the body or body functions can be awkward and shaming.
When others are exposed, as, horribly teased, we can feel vicarious shame.
Anytime we clearly desire something or hold some strong image of ourselves, and cannot display mastery, we feel shame.

John Bradshaw talks poignantly about shame in the original family. He says we have two basis child survival needs: to feel I matter and that my parents are OK: "Parents need to give their children time, attention, and direction, not use them to fill their own need. Use is abuse" (Bradshaw, 1990, p. 42).

He talks about severe shaming in the original family: ". . . the feeling of being flawed and diminished and never measuring up. Toxic shame feels much worse than guilt. With guilt, you've done something wrong; but you can repair that - you can do something about it. With toxic shame there's something wrong with you and there's nothing you can do about it; you ARE inadequate and defective" (Bradshaw, 1990, p. 47).

No animals in the animal kingdom indulge in the kind of recrimination man does. A dog in a fight with another dog doesn't say to himself: "I was just goofing around. I didn't intend to beat him" should he lose. He won't imply the other dog has been taking steroids. He won't get angry at himself for getting out of fighting shape. We humans need to be able to "wipe the slate clean" and begin anew.

In treatment we need to name and understand our toxic secrets. In examining a shaming experience we need to identify what we wanted to occur. How can we make it occur? Is there value in confronting that original parent and receiving aid in clarifying self-image issues?

In children, the destructive behavior parents complain about actually reveals the true self. It releases tension for the child as well. In adulthood you can hear the true self in arguments. People tend to become gruesomely honest in altercations. Some therapists say every argument is really each person saying what about me and my needs?

John Bradshaw explains very well how the shamed person, left with a serious narcissistic wound cannot even mourn the loss. The loss is experienced as catastrophic, and a quick replacement object is substituted. (You can never get enough of what you really don't want.)

If the parental messages were very unsupportive, the child will feel the disturbance. Somewhere, deeply within him, he knows that he IS "OK". The child will begin to reenact circumstances to make the parent love him, or to prove he is loveable and it just wasn't recognized at first by the parents. He fears internally: "They must be right. I really am bad in some way I don't understand." This developing core belief is now "fighting with his intrinsic knowledge that he is "OK". The two core beliefs are now in an internal war inside the child. Very often we can see adults who seem to work hard, want to do well, and then do something odd and foolish "out of the blue" to sabotage the self. The two core beliefs are at war. I am good. I am bad in some way I don't understand.

All clients are at great risk of responding to their injuries with lethargy and depression and/or perverse and even dangerous self-soothing activities.

Common Defense Mechanisms

When we are working in a family, as stated, it can be very threatening to the individuals. Typically, clients will avoid a message or attempt to maintain a negative behavior. The following are some common defense mechanisms people use to avert shame and, or avoid any action.

Denial

The person will flatly reject responsibility. Sometimes he'll plead confusion

Displacement

A person will try to move his responsibility to others: "I'll never be promoted in this bad company no matter what I do."

Identification

The person may idealize another or a group and then try to "merge" with them. "All of my friends who work here have trouble with Mr. Smith."

Intellectualization

The person avoids pain by using abstraction. "My thinking is just so multi-faceted they can't figure out what department to put me in."

Projection

The client moves traits he is ashamed of onto others. "He's so angry, always looking for a fight."

Rationalization

The person justifies negative behavior with statements that seem to be reasonable assessments. "Everyone in this department has trouble with drugs and alcohol."

Reaction Formation

The client takes what he regards as a moral position which may be opposite to what he actually does. "I don't think it's right to drink if you have kids."

Regression

The client reverts back to a prior developmental state. "I don't care if I do have a heart attack, I have to have my greasy burgers."

Repression

The client will not allow negative thoughts to intrude. "I don't remember what he said to me when he broke up with me."

Undoing

The person attempts to cancel out painful experiences. "I don't care if the boss did humiliate me, I'm just going to work harder and hope he doesn't single me out."

All of these defenses will slow up treatment and can be very frustrating for a clinician, but it is important to remember there is a great deal of pain behind all of them. Gently and persistently move clients off of them. Confrontations from the clinician must not replicate the original abuse the clients received at the hands of earlier caretakers.

Don't be fooled by the good actors among narcissists. People can be oddly boastful and arrogant, and then swing to a complete loss of "heart" and be very shy. Truly healthy and happy people don't feel the need to be boastful or bully.

We are beginning to look more seriously at the role of the father. It has been thought for years that mother was by far the most vital parent. That may well be true, and by most clinical accounts if sexual abuse is perpetrated upon the child by the female parent the resultant pathology is more severe than anything done by the male. Perhaps this is because the mother is supposed to be our nurturing person and the bargain feels especially betrayed if she behaves improperly toward the child.

The mirroring from Dad takes an important quality for a number of reasons. He is the "exotic other", the one we're not sure of. He goes out into the world and does _____ to bring home the family's survival. A bit like the mastadon brought to the cave door by the caveman. He has a large power of some sort we are unsure about. We respect him.

Children have an intrinsic sense of their littleness, their inability to solve life problems. How do we keep a house? Where did the car come from? How do we make the food store give us groceries? They know they need these big people.

Mom is the one we're sure of. She's always there (although, sadly, less and less in today's families. We're seeing more and more of the no-parent family). She's the one who spoons carrots into our mouths and wipes and talcs our bottoms. We feel much more sure of her. We know her and she knows us. Winning her respect seems to be much less of a challenge. We want to know what Dad thinks of us. We want to know this all of our lives, perhaps especially so if he is absent.

The parent who does the most caretaking is often dismayed to find he or she receives the most disrespect. The child will more likely disobey and disrespect this parent. It seems unfair to parents, but the "why" is very evident. This is the one he feels loves him. He's sure of this one. He can risk showing his true self. He barely has the other parent and dares not risk crossing him. We see this dynamic very frequently in divorce situations, of course. The "up" side for the caretaking parent is that he/she receives most of the love too.

The father, and his poor treatment of the child can set up some interesting dynamics for a female (also a male but the dynamics are different).

If the father is very domineering, a girl may seek poor treatment, or may altogether withdraw from men in fear of further mistreatment. We recently worked with a woman who picked a very unsuitable man to father her child. Her dad had been very violent, and she wanted a man who would not stay around. The woman may try to permanently "shelve" relationship needs, feeling her safety must take precedence.

If the father is distant and cold the girl may choose males who are cold and are selfish with her. Some psychologists feel this is a struggle to "get love right." Others will say it is a limbic system skewing which will only allow her what is familiar: the coldness.

A doting father would seem to be a good thing, and he is, but he may be using his girl as a little "ally" or confidante. She may become narcissistic and have difficulty giving to her mate in later relationships. She may be spoiled and feel nothing is ever enough, ever good enough, in a later marriage. The man does not measure up to Dad.

If the father is absent she may search through mate after mate all of her life. She may settle for a non-threatening or "inferior" man who will never leave her.

If he is seductive with his child, John Bradshaw calls it "spouse-ifying, " he creates future disaster for her. It is very life-damaging. She may always have trouble with trust issues. She may have serious promiscuity issues or have serious health problems. She will have been thoroughly confused about her true value.

I have spent years working in Domestic Violence programs. I'm convinced poor mirroring (or no mirroring) predisposes women to accept harsh partners. I'm also convinced the father and his treatment of her has the greater bearing on these choices.

We've seen, in the field, some very odd ways for narcissism to play out. One horrifying middle class house had a corner lot in a nice suburb. The lot had many trees and an especially nice dogwood. Inside, the floor was a geological layer literally a foot in thickness. This layer covered every square inch of the floor of this one story home. Doors were frozen ajar where they had been when the pile thickened and obviously had not moved. Some of the layer was spongey in texture, heightening unpleasant imagination. The home was filthy in all areas and very cluttered. Years of newspapers were yellowing on every surface. Yet there was evidence of a love of craft. Someone had lovingly collected lighthouses, dozens of tiny handpainted lighthouses. Food cartons and clothing were everywhere.

The identified patient was the only child, a teenaged daughter of two middle aged, very dirty and overweight adults. We studied the father's filthy long fingernails as he told us he was a chef at a local restaurant.

The daughter had been sexually molested (she remembered a strange black bathtub) by a female neighbor years ago. She would have been about seven years of age. The presenting problem was now her anger and she reportedly would fight with and slap the partially disabled mother at times. She had just returned from a year-long placement at a residential facility.

As we worked on the case we encountered a strange dynamic. The parents who were, to be fair, quite unsightly, taunted the girl about their relationship. They were terribly happy, were so in love, and had been for years. They repeatedly said they doubted if she would ever have anyone, much less a love to equal theirs. The giggled together and held odd little secrets whose purpose seemed to be to "lock the girl out".

We confronted the parents, but their pathology was long established and they simply became angry with us. We then focused on the girl. She had created an elaborate fantasy life around a popular rock group. She wore out the mouth on the paper faces on a poster in her room with frequent kisses. She insisted she was in love, and loved by one of the members of the group. She told her story anywhere and everywhere, causing much negative attention and concern at school. Peers avoided her. Some doctors had written her up as pre-psychotic, a serious diagnosis not usually used on an underage person.

We used frequent and gentle reminders, as well as affective work to help her mourn for the reasonable nurturing parents and the love she did not have. We asked her consistently to come into reality, to be with us in the present. She did not know this rock star, she was sad her parents weren't listening to her and encouraging her. We went over and over this.

We modeled reasonable social behavior for her, taking her frequently to public places. We encouraged her to be less flashy and histrionic. (She was doing "trash dressing" long before it was popular). We helped her to dress her hair and herself is a slightly less eccentric manner (before, her usual garb for school might be an old taffeta wedding dress).

The parents continued to parade their great love to the girl, but by that time she had developed a crush on a classmate and had been accepted into the drama club at school she was not as hurt by their foolishness.

The Marital Relationship

The quality of the parental, marital dyad is very important. We usually do at least a third of our work with the parents and their relationships. If the parent feels very badly he/she has little to give out to the child. The parent is also daily teaching the child by example how to "be" with another. How is power shared, or is it? How is responsibility divided? What role does forgiveness play in a marriage?

Force of will is important in helping the parents make choices. A therapist should let the partners know they have choices. However much they feel old hurts are impinging on their lives people can make a determination within the self: "I will be a loving and generous person". (Or I won't.) They then play out the determination in an intimate relationship with another. The only formula that will work at all is to give the other person permission to follow his "path" in life. Work actively to show the other the support. Make that other person feel "safe". All "paths" have enough inherent problems without the partner also sabotaging success. Promise not to violate the other person's safety, ever, and keep that promise. Keep open communication with the partner so that these issues are always well understood by both partners.

Of course, these suggestions are assuming the partner is not involved in some serious life "violating" behaviors. If he or she is, other options need to be looked at.

Dependence

If the person "needs" the other, all of the person's safety/autonomy is lost. The "needed one" could create harm at any time. This can set up guilt and fear in the needed one; he knows he will sometimes be called the "bad guy" because he didn't fill that need. Will the "needer" totally collapse and crash? Clearly the formula for healthy relationships is for each partner to be relatively healthy and autonomous and to CHOOSE to be with the other. Not to NEED him.

Unmet narcissistic needs of the parent is probably the biggest cause of child neglect. I regard it as even bigger than substance abuse. The parent will put a frantic, limbic system driven search for a mate far ahead of the child and his needs.

A great deal is said against codependence, and it can be very destructive. I regard the codependence so rampant in our culture as a great risk to the child. All needs "pale" next to the codependent parent's search for a partner. More than one parent has told us a relationship is a horror. He knows it's not good for him: but I don't want to be alone. A large issue for the family therapist to deal with is that the parent is exposing his/her most precious thing in life, the child, to the various paramours and lovers. Clients rely on these often total strangers, to have good mental health and total integrity regarding children. Even when their cognitive understanding of the lover tells them the person does not have good integrity, they will often expose the vulnerable child to the person.

We have seen parents accept completely humiliating treatment by a partner because of fears of aloneness. In one situation, a man alternated, in a bigamous arrangement, between two women's homes. Each had his children. When he was pressed in any way by one of the women, he would go to the other immediately and stay. He was not a particularly desirable man in any way. Yet each woman was unwilling to cut ties with him. Of course there was concomitant acting out by the children to protest these dishonest adults. The children were quite ashamed of their mother.

Of course we do need affiliation. Mammals are affiliative by nature. Spiritual teachers will say a person's relationship must be to his god, the highest within that person. To depend upon another, something outside the self, is regarded as unspiritual. This is well and good, probably true, yet it is hard to do so. People feel loneliness very acutely.

The local director of a treatment unit in Allentown has always told his clients: Sex is a WANT. Not a NEED. With every movie and pop song in the culture pushing relationships, solitude, even a "breather" to regroup after a disastrous romance, remains a "hard sell".

Affective work on the individual's sense of "lack" is what is needed. I also think the plain, old-fashioned, force of personal WILL is SEVERELY underutilized in our culture. It is seldom even mentioned any more. Social critic William Bennett is correct on some important issues. We all need to dust off our copies of Ralph Waldo Emerson and read them. There is high value in self-reliance. A successful life and successful parenting demand self-reliance.

We often see adults "shop" for a therapist who will give him or her permission to indulge in corrupt behavior, however. Many, but not all, of these cases "fail" because we cannot get a client to agree to pursue a healthy goal.

I read an interesting book by a Washington, D.C. based psychiatrist. His powerful politician patients were routinely engaged in corrupt, life-violating behavior during the day. It MATTERS what we do. Our actions define who we really are. They tell others what we really think. We cannot violate self and others and feel "happy". The doctor's powerful patients were boring him at night, only seeking pills that would make them feel "happy."

People will try to meet unmet narcissistic needs in many addictive ways. They will grab power, possessions, other partners, substances. None of these efforts will satisfy. The person must face the gaping "hole, " the "lack" within the self and begin to deal with it. Nothing outside the self will help. The best expression used in the old EST training was: "You can never get enough of what you really don't want." What is really wanted is limbic system healing-within the individual.

A Safe Haven?

Childhood should be a safe haven. A child cannot affect finances, the condition of relationships. He does not have the power. He should be protected from adult problems as long as possible. Some part of childhood should be a safe haven so the child can concentrate on accomplishing the very involved developmental tasks he must master in relative calm.

If children do hear unfortunate information a parent can briefly apologize to the child. The parent should assure the child he will make the situation right, if he CAN. A parent should never lie to a child. If a parent does opt to shade the truth in a positive manner, it should at least be remotely possible the parent can handle the situation. A complete falsehood will be too frightening to the child. The lie will be revealed at some point and the parent will seem an uncertain thing. A child desperately needs his parents to be reliable.

We all need to feel we are at least somewhat acceptable and that our parents are acceptable as well (i.e. not too poor, too eccentric, too unattractive etc.)

The greatest gift a parent can give a child is a love of the self. Everything else will result from this self-love. The child will have humor, energy, integrity and courage: all he needs to live a good life.

Fear In Relationships

Our emotional memory bank has registered fear emotions and the causes, and also any fear associated with that general type of situation. If your mother spoke harshly to you when you were two years old and one day stormed out of the house and briefly disappeared around the corner out of sight, potential abandonment may carry a heavy "charge" for you many years in the future. You may pressure your wife any time you fear she will leave you, perhaps pressure her to a self-destructive point, until she does leave. The original fear: I can't survive being left by this person, must be worked out. These deep core fears, if left untreated, are a ticking time bomb that will go "off" in the life. The only question is WHEN.

Imagine the following scenario with a child. A marriage is failing. The couple decides to adopt a child. They have ample resources to care for the boy. The father is very anxious and dependent, possibly suicidal. He is completely ineffectual. The mother is more powerful and has an excellent executive position. She married him because he was warm and posed no threat to her. He would never be mean and shame her as her original family did. She has become bored with him and doesn't respect him now. For the last few years she has conducted an affair with a peer who is more able, as she is. She wants to leave the husband but is concerned about how much damage it may do to her financially. She seems to be scheming how to break him down further so his demands will shrink at the time of divorce. He is immobilized.

The biggest loser will surely be the child. Counter-intuitive to general thought, the best way to treat this family would be to do a good assessment session with the two together and then interview them separately. See if the partners would make a commitment to saving the marriage and really work toward it. If the parents still want the marriage to work, each should then be treated individually, with focus on clearing limbic system blocks. Then, and only then, can they reasonably determine a good course of action for the future. Even if they do separate, the likelihood of vitriolic action that will further harm the boy is greatly diminished.

This adopted child, sensing that something is amiss, perhaps not intellectually understanding why it is amiss, will try to save the family. He will give the parents something new to do: worry about him. As an adoptee, he suffered one abandonment already. He does not wish to suffer another. He will give his parents a common goal: saving him.

Obviously, there's no guarantee this boy's plan will work, but we do see children sacrifice their own safety frequently in an effort to "patch" the family.

Nancy Marshall, M.A.

Parenting Our Parents

It is well known that children of substance abusers will try to assist and stabilize the parent, to great detriment for themselves. They develop what John Bradshaw called "contaminated beliefs" that if they try hard, the world will reward them: "Bradshaw and other therapists have addressed the misplaced loyalty of the child. Children will stay children to heal their parents' narcissistic wounds. The children will commit to never leave their parents as their own parents had done, but to always stay with them and reflecting their 'glory'" (Bradshaw, 1990, p. 16).

Men's movement leader theorist Sam Keen talked of this problem: "Rollo May, in a conversation with me, characterized the problem of the son who is too close to his mother as the opposite of that which Freud presented. The dilemma of the modern son is that he WINS the Oedipal battle against the father and gets Mother. And then he doesn't know what to do with her because she overwhelms him" (Keen, 1991, p. 20)

Erich Fromm

The work of Erich Fromm was always focused on the perfectibility of man. Yet, as Fromm clearly stated, growth is not inevitable. People who do not choose life will choose evilness and self-loss. They are secondary potentialities. Whole societies can choose evilness and self-loss.

Fromm warned in the 1920's that societies which serve the intentions of the few will need to intimidate the many, necessitating inevitable conflict. He said the society must be healthy enough to encourage and foster the growth of each individual. Only then will there be harmony.

The worship of material goods, or an inhumane, abstract God, is the enemy of health and harmony, attempting to put mankind to sleep. I often quote to clients that "There is more to life than obtaining and

78

maintaining objects", as Fromm said. He said that all evil, anti-life societies disappear, as naturally people will not continue to devote themselves to that which is not fruitful. All of our families are profoundly affected by the support, or lack of support in the culture at large for even being a family.

Fromm had very interesting ideas on Co-Dependence: "Alienation as a sickness of the self can be considered to be the core of the psychopathology of modern man even in those forms which are less extreme than psychosis. Some clinical examples may serve to illustrate the process. The most frequent and obvious case of alienation is perhaps the false 'great love'. A man has fallen enthusiastically in love with a woman; after she had responded at first, she is beset by increasing doubts and breaks off the relationship. He is overcome by a depression that brings him close to suicide. Life, he feels, has no more meaning to him. Consciously he explains the situation as a logical result of what happened. He believes that for the first time he has experienced what real love is, that with this woman, and only with her, could he experience love and happiness. If she leaves him, there will never be anyone else who can arouse the same response in him. Losing her, so he feels, he has lost his one chance to love. Hence it is better to die. While all this sounds convincing to himself, his friends may ask some questions: Why is it that a man who thus far seemed less capable of loving than the average person is now so completely in love he seems to be unwilling to make any concessions, to give up certain demands which conflict with those of the woman he loves? Why is it that while he speaks of his loss, he mainly speaks about himself and what has happened to him, and shows relatively little interest in the feelings of the woman he loves so much? If one speaks to the unhappy man himself, at greater length, one need not be surprised to hear him say at one point that he feels completely empty, so empty in fact as if he had left his heart with the girl he lost. If he can understand the meaning of his own statement he can understand that his predicament is one of alienation. He never was capable of loving actively, of leaving the magic circle of his own ego, and of reaching out to and becoming one with another human being. What he did was to transfer his longings for love to the girl and to feel that in being with her he experiences his "loving" when he really experiences only the illusion of loving. The more he endows her not only with his longing for love but also for aliveness, happiness and so on, the poorer he becomes, and the emptier he feels if he is separated from her.   He was under the illusion of loving, when actually he had made the woman into an idol, the goddess of love, and believed that by being united with her he experienced love. He had been able to initiate a response in her but he had not been able to overcome his own inner muteness. Losing her is not, as he thinks, losing the person he loves, but losing himself as a potentially loving person." (Fromm, 1962, p. 53-54).

Still it is foolish to deny that mammals seek affiliation. Animals will cling to one another in perceived danger. As long as our world feels so dangerous to so many people, we will see rampant and destructive codependence and child neglect: "In order to love, the 'other must become a stranger, and in the act of love, the stranger ceases to be a stranger and becomes me.   Love presupposes alienation-and at the same time overcomes it" (Fromm, 1962, p. 57).

In some folk tales, the remedy for dealing with rebellious and dishonest children is to simply love them even more.

Our children are usually teaching us at least as much about life as we are teaching them. We actually are helping each other to expand and grow. Adults are not necessarily that all-wise teacher expounding philosophy to the unknowing. The parent/child relationship is very plastic, always shifting. I like to encourage parents: even if you did it wrong today, there's tomorrow and tomorrow, lots of tomorrows. Try again with renewed vigor. From the moment she appeared, my daughter taught me patience, values, enjoyment skills, and diligence. Not to mention humility.

References

Bradshaw, J. (1990). <u>Homecoming.</u> New York: Bantam Books.

Fromm, E. (1962). <u>Beyond the Chain of Illusion.</u> New York: Simon and Schuster.

Karen, R. (1994). <u>Becoming Attached.</u> New York: Warner Books.

Keen, S. (1991). <u>Fire in the Belly.</u> New York: Bantam Books.

St. Clair, M. (2000). <u>Object Relations and Self Psychology.</u> Belmont, CA: Brooks/Cole.

Talbot, M. (1998, May 24). Attachment Theory: The Ultimate Experiment. <u>The New York Times,</u> 27.

Wiesel, E. (1985). <u>Night Dawn Day.</u> New York: B'Nai Brith.

CHAPTER SIX: THE SUFFERING OF THE CHILD

Wise clinicians are starting to think more in terms of "What's happened to you?" rather than "What's wrong with you?". People behave in a certain way for a reason. They may have arrived at an odd conclusion to justify the behavior, but there was a reason.

We recently completed work on an older teen from a very nice family. She is quite intelligent and involved in foreign language studies and extensive reading. She had completely switched her days for nights, to avoid "the mean people" and "people who stare at me". We began trauma treatment and worked with some shaming that had been done by her father, but this did not seem to really explain the degree of her avoidance. As she improved, we did some very gentle exposure to the school environment: beginning with a quick "pop into" the front hall and home again. Finally, months into the case she revealed that her brother and his friend had sexually assaulted her at age seven. Worse, at seventeen, she was feeling an attraction to him and was deeply ashamed. Upper middle class teens understand the ramifications of revealing an attack such as this and they are extremely reticent to do so. The parents were very shocked and surprised.

Children are suffering very greatly in our society. Their parents come from all socioeconomic groups and races. Most of the parents make a concerted effort to hide their mistreatment of their children. Some are too ill, to "down and out" to even bother with the social convention of appearance of good parenting. And the headlines of our newspapers show us the bad report card our kids are giving us.

Physical Abuse

The loss of power in abuse is a very serious matter. The broken contract is also a very serious matter: a little person should be taken care of by a bigger person.

As stated, children will often not reveal they are being hurt because of the obvious ramifications to the family. They may also fear they will not be believed. Some parents will tell a child this: my word will prevail over yours. All too often it happens. In some situations parents will pull a child out of treatment if abuse history begins to surface. Children also fear even if they are believed, they will not be helped. Sadly, this too happens. What would this do to a child's life philosophy to have this experience?

Young males also greatly fear helplessness. We all fear helplessness, but it is socially less shaming for a female to be a victim. Often the cognition for the boys is: I can't let anyone find out about this.

Very unfortunate beliefs can develop out of abuse: nothing I do matters. How will someone with that core belief try for anything as an adult?

Stefano Cirillo and Paola DiBlasio have done some very interesting work with abusive families. Just as I noted that fear of abandonment was very motivating in Domestic Violence in marriages, they see it at play in violence against children: "Our research has shown us that such child abuse is rooted in fear of loss and abandonment. Psychoanalytical studies underscore the fact that abusive parents tend to react to separation with anxiety and rage . . . If expressed at the right time and place, says Bowlby, such rage operates as a response that can maintain and protect the individual's specific and vital relations, e.g. with a sexual partner, with his or her parents, or with his or her child" (Cirillo & DiBlasio, 1992, p. 111).

Physical hostility can be seen as a way to gain the validation the person feels he or she is not obtaining legitimately in the situation. Interestingly, in treating couples who struggle with violence, we often find women not willing to again engage in sexual activity, or not enjoying it. It may be that on a kinesthetic level, the partner has come to regard the other as a purveyor of only pain, causing unconscious avoidance.

Throughout history people have turned to very dominating power to protect their interests and in the family is no exception.

Unfortunately, it does not feel right to all concerned, and breeds a poisonous resentment, as does all domination.

Cirillo and DiBlasio also agree with other researchers who insist that even very young children are far from indifferent to the suffering in the family. They have seen children in their clinic repeatedly try to alter their behavior to help assuage the family members. Many clinicians, myself included, insist that the beginnings of the return of empathy in any client is indicative of healing taking place in the person. We are returning to our natural state, the one young children have: feeling empathy for others.

We often see children not tell a weak parent of abuse by the other parent. They seem to be protecting the weak parent. I'm not going to give you yet another thing you can't handle or manage. I'll sacrifice myself instead. Of course, a deep resentment goes with this thought, and the child is very sad. Children want and need strong character in their parents and they are quite aware they should not have to go through abuse.

Dr. Bessel van der Kolk of Boston University has done some of the best work with trauma extant, noting that physical beating serves many purposes for the abuser: "Violence serves to punish the other for being autonomous, while also allowing intense emotional contact and the fantasy of repairing the damaged bond" (van der Kolk, 1987, p. 136).

Clinicians can help victims see they have not been in a fair fight. It has not been a fight they asked for. The shame is not in losing, but in winning. Physical abuse teaches primarily that a bigger body can beat up on a smaller body. The child has an intrinsic sense of the unfairness of physicality. I am little. You are large. You are supposed to be taking care of me. Something is wrong with this picture and the one who is wrong is YOU. The world is a very scary place indeed when basis rules can be abruptly upset. Who is safe? The child is always forming his life philosophy, his belief structures: What do I think of the world? Am I safe? Do I like the world? Is there someone bigger here, doing a good job of protecting me?

Domestic Violence

Not enough has been said about the effects of witnessing domestic violence. At any age, all of the messages are bad ones. Someone you love and who says they love you can turn on you at any moment. Your own home is not a place where people can safely express divergent points of view. The only way to gain real power and not to be victimized yourself is to be as brutal as possible. Getting your own way is so important that you need to do whatever you need to do to a "loved" one to prevail. Cowering is trained as a way to survive.

These messages are being encoded into the physical body, as we have seen. Years later, the child will act out of the beliefs formed in these abberational relationships. Women often replicate abuse and pick controlling, harsh partners. Boys may become abusive males, as a role model taught them how to be a man in this way. When the stress level goes up in the present day, as adults, they will behave in the ways that were modeled for them in the original family.

What we have seen clinically again and again is that even if the child is never actually hit, the child is vicariously traumatized by domestic abuse. For a child who is very small a reasonable fear might be that "these two (fighting parents) will kill each other and there will be no one to take care of me. They may turn (and do) on me."

John Bradshaw addressed dysfunctional original families and the pressure they present very wisely. He said the children are allowed to separate from the parents, but only with conditions. The child must always continue to please and honor the parent. The child has an "order" to help take care of the parent's pain. The children will struggle all of their lives to meet these unreasonable demands.

Because there is so much failure in dysfunctional families, they teach children to make a false, uncommitted kind of "try" but not to really succeed. People leave with the cognition: if it appears I tried, I don't really have to do it. There may even be a fear of being punished if the failed parent is surpassed in life. It may be perceived as very disloyal to that parent's hurt feelings to really succeed.

Entitlement in Violence

People can develop a very odd sense of entitlement. It's part of a very elaborate denial system and also part of the "chip on the shoulder" syndrome that we see with so many wounded clients. I have suffered, so the world "owes" me. I'm going to do what I want to others.

A client, a female corrections officer in New Jersey told me the following odd story:

She had been talking with an inmate on the block. He was jailed for a serious assault upon his girlfriend. He explained that they had been out, parked one night. They got into an argument. He became furious and choked her into unconsciousness. She was beginning to be very blue when he realized it could be a serious problem. He gave the girl mouth-to-mouth resuscitation. She came back into consciousness, whereupon she promptly charged him with attempted murder.

The man told the officer "The bitch should have been grateful. I saved her life."

Toward a More Just Society

Erich Fromm said man has needs for belonging and freedom and needs to make efforts toward love and happiness. These drives are inherent in his nature. If the social order oppresses the individual beyond a certain point he will move against the order. It will collapse due to its own corruption and lack of vitality. Our homes will be more just as our society becomes more just. And our society will be more supportive of life when our homes are not so destructive.

Sexual Abuse

The best expression of what sexual abuse is like comes from a poem I saw. It was written by a male sexual abuse survivor who kept his name anonymous.

"I hurt so very bad,
touch me not."

Sexual abuse frightens a person in so many ways. Initially the person lacked the power to prevent a perpetrator from abusing him. He may later feel powerless before all sexual feelings. He may then try rigid control, feeling that all emotions will career uncontrollably into sexuality. This fear of sexual feelings and the attempts to control arousal can actually drive arousal. (I must not think of pink elephants.) The client may fear that he doesn't know what is and isn't appropriate (he may not) in negotiations about sex. He was lied to before by a perpetrator and senses he's lost the ability to have healthy interpersonal experience with sex.

Masturbation

Masturbation to excess, or not done in privacy, can be form of trauma re-enactment. One of the great appeals of masturbation is that it does not involve another (like video games I always say). No social skills are needed. It does not require any self-confidence. Woody Allen goes me one better and says "You don't always have to look your best."

Of course, masturbation can become compulsive and problematical. The fear of the client must be worked with; he/she will need affective treatment. He will need to learn to deal with others in every area of his life in order to have any kind of a useful life. Self-stimulation can be like any other kind of crutch: ultimately not that satisfying. And very isolating.

Different people will respond differently to abuse. Some will react to trauma with flashbacks and other intrusive thoughts. A client may have insomnia. There may be physical symptoms. There may be manic depressive or bi-polar cycles. The client may be hyper-vigilant: I will guard and make sure nothing like this ever happens to me again.

There may be repetition compulsions that serve the purpose of creating a predictable, orderly world for the person and/or keeping him very busy so thoughts don't intrude. The person may be driven to re-enact the trauma, possibly in a "skewed" attempt to resolve it. Some of these rituals gives the person a sense of safety. As we see with anorectics, we control what we can, as we cannot control the mind. Spiritual leader Krishnamurti said because the mind is chaos, we attempt to exercise physical control.

The client may have trauma bonds. He may be drawn to violence or abusive/conflictual ties. Exploitive and dangerous situations may carry an attraction for the client. Wilhelm Reich would say such a person is attempting to "burst out" of depression any way he can. The client may misplace loyalty: cult situations, extreme and shaming co-dependence.

There may be a deep shame with the trauma. The person may harbor an extreme self-hatred and depression. There may be self-mutilation and self-destructive behaviors.

A skewed sense of pleasure may be seen in formerly abused clients. The client may develop some odd arousal patterns, possibly involving high-risk behaviors. The client may become involved in prostitution or even sex-offending. The client may be involved in pain-exchange behaviors.

Many clients opt for blocking the trauma. They turn to substances or excessive sleeping. They are attempting to overwhelm and avoid the residual trauma feelings.

Clients may become involved in extreme fantasizing. Excessive daydreaming may become part of the person's escapes.

Some people become very ascetic. They may become involved in extreme abstinences. Anorexia and agoraphobia are common. They person may neglect self, become addicted to work. Or avoid success and continuously thwart the self. The client may fixate on some odd religious beliefs.

In all trauma bonding, there is hope attached. People waste their time hoping some magic ritual will save them. The victim hopes to get something from the abuser, or a new abuser. Perhaps the "something" is only a "break" this time around. People hope for an apology. It is, of course, a type of magical thinking. The hope itself can be a very deadly thing. If the abuser is dangerous enough, any thing that "glues" a client to him/her is very life damaging.

All of these behaviors, as varied as they can be, are attempts to soothe the self and create safety. Some replaying of events can be an effort to heal. The person would like to replay the event and this time "win", or not be harmed by the event (as they actually were in reality). Some behaviors may be attempts at regaining power or winning revenge.

It is very difficult to deal with any of these behaviors in a loved one. It is frightening and discouraging at times. Some clients can destroy the emotional, physical and financial lives of their loved ones. A family member may feel the acting-out person does not return their love at all. Family members should receive supportive therapy and keep a good network of loving friends whenever they are faced with such serious situations.

It is difficult, but family members must assure the client "I love you no matter what". It is legitimate to not have the person in one's space, but a place must always be kept for the acting -out person in our hearts.

Other Issues

Sex abuse presents different issues for the sexes in many cases. The problem for boys can be that the abuse feels like a thrill. The "thrill" aspect may continue to be a part of the person's sexual life. A large danger for girls is that a girl may be "imprinted" with the idea that only her sexuality matters. It is her only value. Males (and some females) may move from a trauma to a "triumph" in violently projecting the abuse OUT. The person may move into being an offender (Reich's "bursting out"). The helpless feeling is intolerable, especially for males. It is culturally unacceptable.

Our movies and other media do males a great disservice in projecting an image of invulnerability and stressing revenge for wrongs suffered. Some males fear only that they are weak and victimized. Some others wreak revenge and take back the power stolen, sometimes attacking whoever is in the environment. The unfair image of triumph in media hurts us all. It damages our own assessments of ourselves. In reality, whoever you are, you win some and lose some in life. No amount of money or power protects us from this basic human condition. Much relief could be given to our boys and men if the culture would share this fact honestly with them. It probably wouldn't sell a lot of movie tickets, however.

Forgiveness of Abusers

One of the problems with moving to forgiveness in treatment is that there is still such a high level of anger in the client. She/he wants the damaged self honored and acknowledged. The person does not want her/his pain "skipped over". A violation of this order should not simply pass into oblivion. People often feel guilty about verbalizing their real desires for revenge because of religious training. We'd all like to be better than we are. The anger is a part of the stages of mourning for the client. The anger doesn't mean the client will actually harm the other. In fact, if the client can verbalize the hurt in a safe venue, he or she is much less likely to hurt another. The wonderful quick quality of the human mind is a great help. Thoughts continuously move. Our minds will become bored with any stage of experience if we allow them to fully engage with that stage of experience. Feeling ashamed of our thoughts, and truncating them, will cause them to submerge, twist, and grow. It is impossible to keep them submerged indefinitely anyway. The great Fritz Perls used to compare this effort to holding a fully inflated beach ball under the water. Sooner or later that ball will pop up.

A standard exercise that victims of rape and abuse use is to write a letter to the perpetrator, telling him or her how much he's been hurt. Clients can then burn the letter, tear the letter in tiny pieces and flush it way, or otherwise destroy the letter, tear the letter in tiny pieces, and flush it away or otherwise destroy it. Some clients verbalize the desire to throw the letter and the experience with the perpetrator into an unflushed toilet, putting them where they belong – with excrement.

Some of the fantasies of revenge that clients indulge in are quite imaginative. They also demonstrate how strong the feelings of pain still are, and why we can't rush forgiveness.

"I'd make a little slit in his balls and insert lemon juice in them. I would then sew them up again. That way, for the rest of his life, every time he walks, he'd feel how much I hurt. He'd hurt like I do."

"I'd tie his genitalia up in a rope loop, and throw the other end of the rope over a tree branch. Then I'd get over behind the tree and just pull and pull until I pulled them off."

It seems obvious that when people are still experiencing such strong feelings it is very premature to speak in a glib manner about just forgiving and letting it go. Affective treatment should focus on the pain and revenge motivations and accept them as they are without any judgements and help the client process the feelings through, lowering the valence of the emotions. If the client's position is honored in this way, she/he will tire of the anger. The emotion will peak and the client can move forward toward other ideas.

In some ways this is a variation of the admonition: to tell the truth. Let the truth have a life of its own before there is an attempt to disperse it. This does not mean the client is actually going to go out and do something gruesome to another person. Expressing the high level of anger and desire for revenge actually will help to ensure the client does not do anything problematical.

Mother

Generally, clinicians regard sexual abuse done by the mother as the most damaging abuse an individual can suffer, creating the greatest pathology in the life. The image of the all-nurturing mother is very powerful in most cultures, ours included. The greater expectation of the female parent makes betrayal by her far more damaging and frightening. We make mothers more "wise" and "pure" than they actually are.

Frequently children who are being abused engage in magical thinking. In deference to the "mother myth" they think: If my Mom (who is so omnipotent) didn't do anything to help me when I was being abused, she must not have known about it. If the child suspects the mother did know, or knows the mother witnessed abuse of the child firsthand, the child begins to fear: maybe it's because I wasn't worth knowing about.

Shaming

We parents are all too human. Sometimes we are not dealing with a deep pathology, but with a simple embarrassment. We want to appear competent in social settings. An exuberant (or out of control) kid can "blow our cover". We may become very angry, like Lew Schneider: "We'll be over at someone's house, and my child will present me with a broken off piece of someone else's home. I feel like I should walk into the house with a checkbook...and say, 'You know what? Could you just run me a tab? And we'll just settle this up" (Schneider, 1993, Section A, page 2).

A child's poor performance in school can be a shaming thing for the child and for the parent. I have seen parents act out and be especially cruel when they have been embarrassed by their child.

In their own upset state, parents say things that teach a child that what he is defective. Not that he did something bad, but that his very beingness is defective. John Bradshaw has said that anything that violates a person's sense of self should be considered violence. People are taught how to be abused. They duck and cover and try to hold on until the abuse is over. We see people in adult life who "hunker down" in what we regard as cowardice or denial. It may very well be an early survival mode, learned in times of great pressure for the child. They learned long ago they CAN'T protect themselves. Children are being scarred by their parents. The scalding messages say: In your essence you are not good. It's not only what you've done that is not good, but you yourself will never be good. You are no good. Parents subtly teach their children not to be important, not to dare to be close, not to grow up, to love only me and not others, to not pester me, to not have any problems, to not be sane, to do succeed, to don't succeed, to don't be at all, to not be physically well, to not overshadow me.

The child, for his part, is saying: Hear me. I want you to listen to me. Love me. I'm your child. Be interested in me. Love me. Please love me. These childhood pleas are often shouted out by even sixty-year-old me, years later, in therapy.

Shaming can also occur in the way a child is treated in everyday matters. A woman in therapy recalled, at her age of eight years, she wanted the last Fudgecicle. Money was not an issue in the family and the family could afford Fudgecicles. Her mother shamed and scolded her, then ate the Fudgecicle herself. What message does that send the child?

Current Safety Issues

The most important thing any clinician must attend to in any situation is the safety of the more vulnerable family members. We must help the individual suffering in the moment, at the risk of "goring someone's ox." People may pull family members out of treatment. Schools may object. Government systems may be angered. But if we don't help the vulnerable person in the moment we ourselves are corrupt. If we don't help, we must seem like some odd collaborators, enablers in the abuse.

Erich Fromm said man is highly adaptable, but he will not forever tolerate conditions that violate his very basic needs. We have needs for freedom, expression, happiness, love and belonging. These needs are deeply inherent in our nature. The social order, or a given marriage or family, may oppose these needs for a time, but it will not feel right to all concerned. The situation will eventually collapse because of its own lack of vitality and destructiveness. Our families will be supportive when the culture is supportive, and the culture will change when our families change, one by one, in therapy.

Nancy Marshall, M.A.

References

Cirillo, S. & DiBlasio, P. (1992). Families That Abuse. New York: W.W. Norton.
Schneider, L. (1993, June 12). Famous Faces, Express-Times. Section A, Page 2.
Van der Kolk, B. (1987). Psychological Trauma. Washington, D.C.: American Psychiatric Press.

CHAPTER SEVEN: CURRENT SAFETY ISSUES

Good clinical work has to have a "watchdog" quality to it, like it or not. We look like fools and worse if we don't attempt to intervene when the strong are attacking the weak. It is preferable to not be involved in a case at all than to heighten the cynicism of an already suffering person.

Issues of Safe Custody

The same principle applies when a child is in a truly unsafe placement, even with a natural parent. If we cannot actually alter the situation, the success of any type of psychological help will be greatly diminished. What are we really offering if the everyday circumstance is fraught with risk and remains so?

With warring parents it's important to determine what is actually happening. A good assessment should include an interview with both parents. It's common that one or both have an agenda of making the other one the "wrong one" and that this revenge tactic will completely impede all quality treatment.

Sexual Abuse: The "Vampire Bite"

Occasionally a good Family-Based Treatment assessment will yield the very unpleasant fact that sexual abuse is currently occurring in the home and an underaged person is not being protected. Children who have been victimized may victimize neighbors and siblings, usually with the most powerful person (generally, but not always the older person) victimizing a less powerful person, and so on down the "pecking order." Parents must be very careful to monitor older foster children or even relatives. Very often the histories that come with foster or even adoptive children are woefully incomplete. A severe abuse can take place in a matter of a very few minutes and we adults are not always so alert as we like to think we are. A child will often not tell an adult of a sexual abuse because it is so shaming, he is afraid of the perpetrator, or he may be trying to protect the family from "bad news".

Neglect

We have seen many cases which were labeled counseling cases which were actually neglect cases. Sometimes the overburdened Child Protective Services agencies will triage cases and not deal with neglect. We see children whose teeth have been so rotted out that it makes our own teeth hurt to behold them. How can a child in this condition care about our counseling?

We see, because of illness or addiction in a parent, many cases in which a young child is actually the one in charge of the family. Eight year olds will fry up an inadequate dinner in a filthy setting and feed younger children. That older child becomes understandably angry and resentful, but will usually remain fairly dutiful.

We had a case in which both parents were doing a suicide by "millimeters." The father had severe kidney disease, but remained very overweight, eating and drinking things that exacerbated his health problems. Two or three times a year he would leave his permanent perch on the sofa downstairs and go into the hospital where he nearly died. He would be "pieced" back together to return home. This father, when pressed, expressed discouragement that his alcoholic wife did not come back from her diner job at night.

She was known to be cheating on him. She did not want to come back and be his wife and the children's mother because he was so ill and not committed to taking any care of his health. It was no fun to be home. We held both parents responsible, but were ultimately not able to budge them. They were unwilling to work on the causes of their individual pain. The three children were "quite out of luck." The oldest boy was doing what housework was done. He did not take his schoolwork at all seriously and was labeled Oppositional Defiant Disorder. Sadly, this neglect did not rise to the level of government intervention. I often thought how stupid our "nice talk" must have sounded to him. Then again, being an eight-year-old, he probably told me a few times how stupid it sounded.

Death or Jailing of a Parent

Any absence of a parent is very serious. Emotions are not reasonable. Our adult emotions are not reasonable. THEY are three years old. How can we expect more from a small child? We don't care why a loved one is absent. No answer makes "sense." We can know intellectually, but not care at all in our limbic systems. All I know is you're not here. I'm hurting. If I were a good child (wife, etc.) you would be here. If you loved me you would be here.

People, including children, often will not verbalize these thoughts. They know the thoughts are not rational. They're ashamed of the thoughts and of the circumstance itself: my important person has left me. The exposure is painful: I need and clearly want something I can't get. The unmet needs are an embarrassment to the person. It is the essence of shaming to be seen to want something badly and then be so "defective" it can't be obtained. The exposure is unbearable.

Careful affective work must be done for all individuals if the person does return. The return will not resemble a glowing Disney script. Feelings are hurt and they will have to be dealt with.

More will be said about healing from the loss of a death in the Treatment Chapters.

Failures in Other Systems

All systems are only as good as the integrity of the people managing them. Our Children and Youth, Juvenile Probation and Court systems can act with integrity or malevolence. The single greatest heartache of my career is the understanding that adults will act cruelly and ruin a young person's life. Often the situation is just an impersonal sadism. Wilhelm Reich was very interested in the "little man" in power in systems and wrote extensively on the subject. I can certainly understand hatred and anger. Even revenge. The impersonal cruelty is a strange and harsh thing to behold. Most of the people acting improperly in official roles are quite aware the average person doesn't have the political knowledge or resources to seriously challenge the power in these groups.

Any clinician who finds himself working for a corrupt system has no real choice but to do the best he can while in the job, but to leave the position as soon as possible. The effect on one's clinical work and very soul is completely corrosive.

Of course, it must be said, there is much well-intended work done in these systems as well. Buddha's great admonition was to HAVE GOOD INTENT.

Schools

If a school wants to assist a clinician in the treatment of a child it can be invaluable. The school is such a large part of the child's environment. If the school day is very ego dystonic and shaming, it makes the treatment job very difficult. Vicious, unchecked peers are among the greatest hazards present in our schools today. Adults send the message by not dealing with severe bullying that they too are afraid of the bully. People in schools run the gamut from very wise and resourceful mentors to vicious shaming bureaucrats. It would be helpful if "burned out" teachers (and therapists, too for that matter) would leave their respective fields and not inflict harm on vulnerable young people. A wise clinician will always sharpen diplomacy skills and attempt to enlist the school's aid whenever possible. Parents must also gauge carefully when their advocacy helps and when it hurts in a school situation.

We are currently working with a teenager whose vice principal encourages youths to give him information on peers to save themselves from disciplinary action. Kids have been badly beaten after school hours for giving information. I find this, and the lessons it is teaching, truly horrifying.

Treatment Providers

Other treatment providers also run the gamut from very wise and skillful to coercive and shaming. We saw a horrible example possible of competitive zeal run amok, later ruining a child's life.

The client was fourteen years of age. He had been sexually abused by adult males four times before he was twelve years of age. He was even victimized by a foster father. Finally he began telling his mother what was happening and begging not to be returned there. He was about twelve years of age at that time.

His mother was not a strong person, and not surprisingly, her original family history was very difficult. She heard her mother attempt to stop her father from drowning her sister in an upstairs bathtub. (The mother was successful, and the sister had lived.) She had learned to run in a zig-zag line from her house as a girl in case her dad fired shots out at her. This woman was not "on the ball" as a parent, and her son was badly harmed. We won't be able to talk her into being a good parent. She needs individual therapy for trauma.

As the adult, and our client's mother, she did pull her son from the foster father. The boy was put by well-intended county officials into a treatment program for sexual offenders. (He had made inappropriate gestures towards another child.) This treatment was based on a strict behavioral model. The client was to recognize his impulses and immediately attempt to deal with them. The clients worked in groups and were to keep diaries regarding the number of sexual impulses they had in a given day. The boy had been working for six months or so in the program to no great effect when we were brought in to try to make some difference in his continued sexual gestures and inappropriate interpersonal comments in school. He had not actually offended against another in over a year. I assigned him my best male clinician, who began to do affective work for the boy and allow him to mourn his lost childhood and all of the abuses he had suffered. We helped him express through the body (with EMDR and Thought Field Therapy) and verbally how hurt, angry, and overstimulated he felt. The school and the parents began to see improvement in his behavior. We also did do the affective work for the trauma with the mother.

The other facility began to feel annoyed by the reported improvement in his behavior and went "gunning" for him. They felt a huge obligation to prove our work wrong. Arguments ensued in meetings. The other company felt you first work with the bad behavior and try to stop it. We insisted he needed to simultaneously mourn the pain and work with the bad behavior, or he would not feel good enough to do what was being asked of him in terms of self-control. The other company successfully scared a local judge on the basis of behavior the boy had committed the year before. We argued in court to no avail that it only served to fuel discouragement and anger to punish the boy for behavior he did a year ago, but sex offender cases appear to judges in their bad dreams. The other company argued he was entering fewer sexual impulses in his diary, was lying. We felt sure it was because he actually was having fewer impulses, felt better, and that the school and parents had also seen concomitantly improved behavior at school and at home. Our patient was more empathic, and generally less angry and depressed by their reports.

Off he went to Diagnostic placement, where he behaved very badly. Additionally, this poor boy contracted tuberculosis at the facility. The boy was intelligent. He was in court and heard the "firefight" over him; he knew he was railroaded. His County worker and I talked for years about this case and how frustrated we were at the way our hands were tied and, most of all, about the horrible results obtained.

PART II: TREATMENT

CHAPTER EIGHT: TELL THE TRUTH

The most vital first step in all healing is to tell the truth. It can be painful, it can be embarrassing, it can be saddening, but only the truth begins the healing journey. Wilhelm Reich taught that a lie, or an avoidance, was a shrinking away UNTO DEATH. A lie is bad for the bioelectrical life of the organism.

One of the strangest contributions of the Nazi Germany government was the "Big Lie." The government evolved a theory that the truth was unimportant. It was thought the people were so stupid, the truth so feeble, that if a blatant lie were repeated often enough, by enough "authority, " that it would supplant the truth. The Big Lie would become much more important than the truth.

Everywhere in our culture we see the cynical use of the Big Lie. Yet the truth will well up again and again, even though it may take time. THE TRUTH IS NEVER NOT TRUE.

One of the sad, and sometimes humorous things we encounter in therapy is that people request therapy, and then hope we do not know what we are doing. Or if we do know what we are doing, we will be unwilling to disturb anyone by telling the truth about what's going on in the family. They are looking for approval of a corrupt situation. They would like for the Identified Patient's bad behavior to stop and for pressure to ease in their households without making a change in themselves. In private therapy people will abruptly end the treatment. In our particular unit, that can be more difficult to do in the therapy. I particularly dislike seeing the public dollar used to support corrupt situations when there is so much genuine unmet need.

Tell the truth. Only the truth heals. It is the first step toward wellness. No matter how ugly or painful the truth is, it contains the seeds of healing. One of the best "weapons" we have in treatment is that only what's true is true. The body, being an organism fitting squarely into the rest of nature, cannot be fooled by The Big Lie. Illness and stress will result if people try to continue to force The Big

Lie. Eventually all dishonest scenarios will break down in one fashion or another.

The need to tell the truth can be seen simply from a common logistics point of view. If you need to get from Point A to Point B, you must first admit to being at Point A. How else can you plan your traverse?

The famous psychiatrist Fritz Perls talked of supression as so going against the natural order of the universe that it is like continuously trying to hold a beach ball under the water. The moment the guard is let up, the ball pops up.

Beginning to tell the truth identifies "where the mind is at." There must then be a change in the limbic system, a healing. In order to be healthy, we need to be able to interrupt the machine-like chatter of our own minds. Managing the mind is the stated goal for enlightenment in the Eastern religions. Christianity speaks often of managing the mind. Eastern religion goes so far as to speak of the mind as a wild tiger, which, unless tamed, will turn and rend you.

I think the future of mental health treatment will stress much more involvement and taking of responsibility for self on the part of clients. Therapists will be more like good, careful coaches, but the client will have to work in a determined and dedicated manner on his own behalf and will be expected to do so.

DENIAL

Denial is a good TEMPORARY measure to get a person through a difficult time. It should not be kept as a permanent pattern of coping with life. There is no real value in lying about what is. Reality will keep intruding and calling your attention anyway. Often the delay will allow the burbling situation to become worse, then requiring a much more vigorous response. Mr. Blanton talks of telling the truth as a first step in healing: "You admit that who you are is not who you have been pretending to be" (Blanton, 1991, p. 85).

My Experience

I know from personal experience the high degree to which people try to deal with uncomfortable situations by denying they are suffering. My stated (not unconscious) core philosophy was "I can handle it." After all, I was a military man's daughter. I also suffered from a chronically stuff neck and was often in the chiropractor's office. I always thought it was the work I did at a drawing board while I worked as a commercial artist. Finally, in the middle of a psychological seminar I said to myself: "I'm sad. I feel like it's raining shit - all the time." A few hours after this honest, clear statement, while I was lying on my bed resting, I suddenly felt jolts of electricity going through my neck and shoulders. My heart fluttered wildly, frightening me. The whole experience really scared me. Suddenly my neck began to spasm. When the spasms ended, my neck was no longer stiff. In fact, my neck has never really been stiff since then. I am convinced that my miraculous physical healing was brought on by my finally telling the truth. I had been steeling my neck and back against the raining blows to come. It was going to rain shit.

Many Small Lies

We see evidence of not telling the truth everywhere in the culture. Clients must not be allowed to bury or obfuscate the truth. For example, a client should not be allowed to say: "I lost it." Losing your temper is a choice. The person must be made to tell the truth: "I gave myself permission to lose my temper hoping to achieve some effect or change in a situation." That's the truth. NOT "I lost it."

Help clients suspend their own judgements about themselves. Those postures we take for the sake of protocol are huge impediments to treatment. The first step to managing the mind has always to be to TELL THE TRUTH. Assess the mind where it is now. What is my mind now saying? NOT what should it be saying.

Dr. Nathaniel Branden worked often with this principle. He created ways of discovering what the mind is thinking and then coping with it: "There is an exercise that I give to therapy clients today that I wish I had known about then. The course of my life over the next decade or so might have been different. If for two weeks I had sat at my desk each morning and wrote the following incomplete sentence in my notebook: 'If I bring a higher level of consciousness to my relationship with Barbara' and then wrote six to ten endings as rapidly as I could, without rehearsing, censoring, planning, or 'thinking', I would have found myself making more and more conscious explicit, and inescapable all the deep reservations I had about this relationship as well as my process of avoidance and denial" (Branden, 1994, p. 82).

Here, Branden is offering a simple, do-try-this-at-home method of looking at our belief systems and understanding how they are tripping us. The key is being willing to look. He doesn't have to show his notebook to "Barbara, " in fact, he should not. Just doing the sentences will reduce the pressure enough for him that it is very possible he will be more conscious in the relationship. Our egos are very good at darting around and hiding their true motivations. Encourage clients to look. There is nothing so horrible, so dark, that it can't be dealt with: "I cannot forgive myself for an action I will not acknowledge having taken . . . If I refuse to accept that often I live unconsciously, how will I learn to live more consciously? I cannot overcome a fear whose reality I deny" (Branden, 1994, p. 93).

Telling the Truth Helps Us Identify Belief Systems and Work With Them
Any time, and every time that we can change our thought in the moment, and move toward a thought that is more positive and supportive, it is a tiny chip in the block of core belief. These tiny "chips" can add up and give us strength. The core beliefs have been compared to a large block of ice. If one diligently chips and chips away at it, eventually an air pocket or chip in the block will cause it to split and sink. It is a matter of steadily applying proven techniques to change dysfunctional core beliefs.

Telling the truth will help us not amplify situations. We tend to assign (VERY quickly, that's why it seems so real) arbitrary meanings to events. Our primitive brains then respond to the threat with far too much amplitude for what is actually taking place. The great Issac Singer, who lived through World War II in Poland adopted a good standard for whether or not the mind can regard an event as a tragedy: "Will little children die from it?" If not, it wasn't a tragedy, said this great writer, and we need not assign such amplitude. This is true of even the most mundane circumstance. If I need to cross the busy highway I live on, I have a better chance of making it to the other side if I am not responding with tremendous fear from the past, tremendous anxiety, but rather, feel calm, and use my senses in the present, judiciously, to check the road before I move.

Our thoughts do have power. If we continue to dwell on a thought, it takes on more and more reality for us, through the practice. That is why it's so important to monitor our thoughts and keep working with them, not letting negative thoughts take hold. If they have taken hold, we need to work with vigor to alter them.

Fear

A common miscalculation in our culture is that fear is a friend and assists us. Actually, it debilitates us, and cause us to give away the power we do have. We need to use common sense and respect danger and threats when they do appear. But we need to face them (tell the truth), and make the best possible assessment of how we want to approach it and deal with it. If I need to cross a busy street, I am always better off assessing the traffic, and making my move in calmness. It certainly is not helpful to be very fearful and remember every tale I have ever heard of someone who was hit by a car. This is why simple denial is so harmful. We need to use our perceptions to have a good life. We have five good senses for a reason. To not use them and our good cognitive common sense is reckless.

If you want to regard fear as your friend, deal with the crisis first, and let your knees buckle later.

Guilt

When we are busy feeling very guilty, we are living in the past. We are not taking the course of action we need to be taking in this moment. It is really another avoidance or another denial. Even if something that will act against our good has been done, it is already done. We've done a bad thing. It's in the past. It is better to tell the truth: I did this bad thing, make reparation if you can, and move ahead into the future, which is the only place you can live.

People are preoccupied with their own survival. Surviving is the first job of the organism; our primitive brain was to protect the survival. For example, people may praise a powerful person, hoping to curry favor for a future need. Powerful people may send off a signal that they only want praise in their experiences. Often leaders are surrounded with people afraid to give anything but praise. They are interested in their own future survival, of course, not what will really assist the leader. The moment the powerful person loses his power, he will find his "fans" are gone. We need to have a sense of what is true and belief in our own worth. We don't want to face life cowering, with a profound and grave vulnerability. We frequently see this type of "leader-led" dynamic in a family, in a job situation, everywhere in life.

Motivations

Tell the truth. Look carefully at motivations. The Buddha said Desire is the Enemy. Desire can go out of control and cause a person not to respect his life or the life of others. Desires are also a force for good; they cause us to take action. It is a question of balance; life can still be good if a given desire is not met. Again, it is the amplitude we assign to the desire in our thoughts.

Love

Tell the truth about love. We have to allow another to love us, or not. To make us happy with his actions and words, or not. We are not the puppetmaster, in control. We are not God. We must respect the life and will of the other and let him follow his own will, his sense of his highest good. If it is his highest good to love us, so much the better. Of course, it is possible to coerce others for a time, and subvert their wills, but it will never feel right and there will eventually be a cost to this behavior.

If we are frustrated with certain desires, we may focus constantly on the fact that the desire was not met. We can focus so much on how the desire was not met that we feel empty. We have a massive deep "hole" in us. We then try to fill it with power, money, alcohol, etc. The old EST training used to say: "You can never get enough of what you really don't want." We need to tell the truth about our desires and then keep them in balance. All of the world's great religions speak of balance. If we get far enough out of balance we will actually force our goal away. If we are in balance, and using our senses and cognitive ability, we may take action that can be useful.

What sweetheart will love us more if we are very controlling and jealous? If we press him and make him suffer, will that enhance love? Or will we force our goal away? If we are controlling and vindictive, will that make us successful in our roles at work? Or will people shy away from us without explanation or rage back at us and then escape? Will they wait for an opportunity to take revenge on us? We need to tell the truth about motivations and keep ourselves in balance.

Telling the Truth in Difficult Times

Face the problem squarely: this is what is happening. Try to see how you might deal with the problem. It certainly may not be welcome, but the chances are, you do have the personal resources to handle it. You may not handle the crisis as skillful as is shown "in the movies." But you will face it. If you have it in your life, you must handle it. Tell the truth. It's bad, I'm scared, or whatever it may be. But see the possibility of handling it. Don't let your ego reduce your skill in handling it by telling you horror stories about your abilities. It will only reduce your inherent skills. A useful exercise is to go over the many events in your life that seemed overwhelming and terrifying. Write the events or crises down. Then reflect upon them and realize you DID handle them. You handled them awkwardly or stunningly well. You handled some after delay, some not. But you still exist. You survived. You must have handled them. Keep this list and refer to it when you are frightened anew. You DO have resources and abilities.

We give our power away too easily. I often describe to my staff the common behavior we see in clients and ourselves. The person sits in the corner, curled up, with his thumb in his mouth. He's having an existential "tantrum" that he has something unwelcome in his life to handle. He hopes that if the tantrum is big enough, "God", or some magic, will feel sorry for him, or be frightened by his anger, and "swoop down" and rescue him from the problem. It isn't going to happen and he needs to stop wasting his time and claim his power. He needs to tell the truth: "I hate it, and here it is, in my life. And I'm going to handle it, somehow." The first step: tell the truth. Taking positive action does take courage. Often we are so discouraged we fear nothing will work. I like this suggestion from Arnold Patent: "For those who still have doubts about the law of cause and effect, I have the following suggestion. Just assume that it does apply. There is no way you can hurt yourself. For if the law does exist, you gain the benefit of believing it. If it doesn't, you lose nothing. Not believing it means that anything can happen to you at any time. There is no way to protect yourself against such a situation, no matter what you do or believe. At least you know you haven't failed to improve the quality of your life because you didn't give yourself to the chance to improve it" (Patent, 1984, p. 46).

Telling the truth, and not criticizing and frightening yourself takes work, but it can be done. Useful ideas can come from many different sources, and I do not have a problem reading from spiritual literature. Emmanuel's Book offers the following advice: "Do not criticize yourself because in darkness you could not see" (Rodegast & Stanton, 1985, p. 101).

The book talks movingly of the frightening experience of change:

"Expansion there are moments of great insecurity.
Let me offer you an analogy.
When you take your foot from one rung of a ladder
To put it on the next.
There is nothing for you foot to stand on
For that brief moment.
If you were to focus all of your attention
And identify all of your reality
With the sole of that suspended foot
You would truly be in a state of terror.
You do not see
The hands holding the sides of the ladder
Or the other foot that is firmly planted
On the rung beneath"
(Rodegast & Stanton, 1995, p. 113).

Tell the Truth/Don't Tell the Truth

Dr. Arthur Janov talks of the process involved in obfuscating the truth in the original family in a clear way: "But it is not just Pain that is the cause of psychosis; it is also the degree of disconnection from it. Disconnection forces us to deny what really happened and substitute something different. The child whose parents tell him repeatedly that their violent fights are 'normal' and shouldn't upset him must then come up with another reason for feeling so desperately upset. There is an inverse relationship here: the less validation the child receives for his feelings in the context in which they occur the more disconnected and bizarre the 'reasons' for the feelings will become. Thus, if the child is forced to deny his real fear of his parents he may then transform it into a fear of his teachers. If that fear is still discounted and belittled by his parents-'Oh, Johnny, that's just ridiculous, your teachers won't hurt you'-the child will be forced to search even further for 'reasons'. He may then come up with "I can't go to school because I'll die if I use the toilets.' And so on, until there is a thoroughly distorted mind. And all because the child's original rightful feeling of fright and terror in response to parental violence was flatly denied" (Janov, 1970, (Primal Therapy), p. 186-187)

Janov is expressing the need to tell the truth as the first step toward true healing. He talks about the bursting forth of the truth against the repressing person's will: "The person who is suddenly thrust into consciousness by night terrors is experiencing first-line energy bursting upward through the repressive barriers. And usually the nightmare just before the abrupt awakening is characterized by first-line concomitants: inability to catch one's breath, a crushing or squeezing sensation, a feeling of drowning or suffocation, a trapped feeling and the sensation of imminent death" (Janov, 1970, p. 193).

It is easy to see Dr. Reich's ideas about "bursting forth" rediscovered.

All of us fear a loss of meaning in our lives. We fear death. We fear living a life without meaning. We are afraid of being alone. Existentialism teaches us that you create value by creating value. We can declare: this is what my life is about, what my "mission" is, and do it. Value inexorably follows this declaration. We would all benefit from letting go of narcissistic images. My mission can be to repair shoes in a really careful and skillful way and to provide friendly service and to know my neighbors. I don't have to be a 007 super-spy or the President of the United States. The truth is, we all want, very badly, to matter, and we all can.

If we will take care of what we have right before us in a responsible way, greater freedom and more "interesting" assignments will come. Responsible people begin to get more exciting assignments.

Young clients often tell us they are going to be a veterinarian or a doctor, yet are failing math right now, and not willing to work on assignments to develop skill. We want our rewards laid out for us immediately in this culture. Do you really want a veterinarian working on your dog, or a doctor working on you, who didn't do his assignments? Commitment is not a torture, it can help set the meaning of our lives.

We cannot get understanding a priori. We can't get iron-clad guarantees our efforts will yield exactly what we want. We have to be willing to make an effort on faith.

In the twenties and thirties, Dr. Erich Fromm talked about filling the "void" of our narcissistic wounds with material things. He said there was more to life than obtaining and maintaining objects. We see throughout our culture that we are willing to shame individuals, using their narcissistic wounds, into buying what they don't need, can't afford, and may even be harmed by. We are too willing to exploit each other on our jobs. Anything that hurts any family, hurts us all. How can we be so sure our neighbor's child will not be next to our child in school? If we harm that neighbor, he may be ill enough to create a tire that will explode on the highway and kill my beloved.

Love

Intellect and emotion are created by separate neural systems, causing the chasm between reason and feelings in our lives. The limbic brain, shared by all mammals, holds all emotions, instincts and hormones. It only feels, it does not evaluate. This is why we see smart people making stupid decisions.

Good affective work can assist with this limbic system damage. The client must return to the origin of the pain, usually the original family, and he must be able to tell the truth about what he experienced.

Bradshaw says we do not get the mirroring we wanted and needed. We did not feel unconditional love, impeding our ability to trust. We then see people with insatiable cravings and who need to be constantly validated. The cry for validation can be so intense that the person seems to feel he will perish without it.

Repeated shaming will drive depression. Repeated reminders of one's inadequacies can become paralyzing for a person. We see this often in school failure situations. We see students decide they cannot face another humiliation in life, and thus, will not try at all in school.

Telling the truth about this shaming can be difficult for the family to hear. But the self is hurt, badly hurt. Emotionally mutilated. This self wants its genuine pain honored, looked at, understood. It doesn't just want some glib therapist, or teacher (or partner or family member) to pass it right over: "The past is the past. You need to let it go."

Religions correctly stress forgiveness to help honor the life still left in the person. But the injured person feels a need to not "jump the gun." People are asked to emotionally move to forgiveness they don't yet feel. Truncating the process breeds fear and resentment. Only the truth is true-not what should be true. Our emotions are rude, "three-year-olds." They don't care what religion says we should feel. They feel what they feel.

Another forgiveness issue is that the person often doesn't yet feel fully safe, even though he actually may be safe. Forgiving may feel like giving permission to do it again. That would be scary to anyone who has been victimized.

When I worked at a rape crisis center in New Jersey I was often amazed at the "punishments" clients imagined in their journals for perpetrators of sexual abuse. Polite, middle class people who would never harm anyone were encouraged to give vent to their angry feelings as a way of moving into another place emotionally about the event. It was stressed that dreaming of the punishments was a state in the healing and we would never actually do these things.

Shame

Shame has a quality of the unexpected. We never know when it will be coming. We are suddenly "invaded" by the feeling and overpowered. Usually in shaming experiences there is an incongruity between our image of ourselves and what has taken place and what it reveals about us. This disturbance of our self-image can come from a seemingly trivial incident.

Shame can come suddenly from the thwarting of an expected positive response. Our "needs" have been exposed, and then some entity or circumstance refuses to fill the needs. A rush of shame will follow this experience. The more we expected a certain response, the greater the pain engendered by the denial.

A heedless dismissal of our "offerings" can be especially shaming. Any time we have created something, or made something, we want very much for it to be accepted by others. Shame will always cause us to feel less comfortable at home and in the world. We have missed an imaginary goal. Everyone has seen us miss. The greatest pain comes from the high expectation of reward that is thwarted.

Behind a sudden rush of shame is a deep fear of abandonment. My littleness and inadequacy has been so exposed that others will rush away from me in disgust. Of course these are the most difficult issues to tell the truth about because of their inherently embarrassing quality.

Poverty and Shame

"People talk about poverty and the poor like it's so easy not to be poor. But I know a different story. It takes great sacrifice and talent to work your way out of poverty. My mother used to make all of her own clothes. You couldn't raise four boys on her salary and afford to buy dresses to wear to work. When we were young, she used to make our clothes, cut our hair and make toys for us out of cereal boxes. All he life she sacrificed for us. She put off getting her college degree and her master's degree until we were grown and out on our own.

"And you know what? We hated being poor. We loved our mother but we ruined her Christmas every year with our tears of disappointment at not getting exactly what we wanted. I couldn't help but be angry when my shoes had holes in them there was no money to buy new ones. And I couldn't help but stare angrily when I needed money to go on a school trip and there wasn't any money to be had.

"And while there was much love in our family, being poor strained our loving bonds. We had to blame someone, and my mother was the only target…And she would come home to four boys with their hands out, angry because we wanted something, needed something she could not give" (Canada, 1998, p. A-19).

Tell the Truth/Blame

Blame disempowers us. It keeps us lost in conflict and heightens a sense of doom. The most valuable thing you can think is: o.k. This has happened. What can I do now? Telling the truth would involve admitting the thing has happened and it will help us to admit it and move forward with some plan of action instead of flailing about denying it has occurred.

Anger

Anger is more socially acceptable for all of us than fear. Especially for males, who have been weaned on false media images of male strength, it is hard to acknowledge fear is what we are feeling. If I feel afraid, and deeply ashamed, and especially if I am publicly exposed, I may move quickly to place a blame on someone else. Like all denials, the lie does not allow us to correct any errors we have actually made. The lack of truth prevents us from being as effective as we could be. This kind of projection is rampant in current American politics and throughout our companies and institutions.

It takes a very healthy person to say, wearing his red face, I miscalculated on that. I was wrong. And a healthy group, which is able to resist the temptation to grab and excoriate a scapegoated individual, thereby projecting away its own shame.

Tell The Truth/Mothers and Daughters

There is a tacit understanding that the daughter will be like her mother. A mother can feel threatened if she is a limited person and is faced with a confident daughter who is able to seize opportunities and move forward in the world in a way only the mother's husband and brothers have been able to. It inherently makes the mother WRONG. The mother may also feel a vicarious fear and worry that her daughter will be safe in a world she never dared to traverse.

This dynamic is further complicated by the fact that the daughter is a source of great pride for the mother, and she is genuinely happy for her child and her success. (Of course, we see this dynamic everywhere with fathers and sons as well.) No wonder mothers and daughters have difficulty sorting out these conflicting feelings about each other.

Many theorists feel the driving force behind eating disorders is the pre-adolescent girl's discovery that a "woman's place" is still not necessarily a good one in our society. She may be severely constricted by her male partner in a relationship. She may also feel that life should have a balance and although work can be wonderful, it's nice to have a relationship. Many latency aged girls are shocked to discover they may be facing altogether different pressures than their male buddies and that they may be more difficult to resolve. They may want to avoid developing into a woman altogether (anorexia), or try desperately to fit some model they think will not arouse too much ire from the world at large (bulimia, overeating).

Tell The Truth/Men

Psychologist Warren Farrell has been helpful in elucidating issues between men and women. Men are showing their love for their families by the way they materially provide for them. This providing has become more difficult for blue collar and even some white-collar men. Men have a large fear of stumbling in this competition. This fear is projected onto others they can name as "losers, " who are also losing this race. This fuels prejudices and class prejudices of all types. Advertising increasingly drives us all to consume more and more goods with television presenting an image suggesting that all others have these goods, driving fears of inadequacy in the breadwinners. Inadequacy is something they cannot tolerate. It recalls the shaming in the original family. It "must" be projected out.

Some of the spiritual writers have done a good job of clarifying some of the pain men are feeling: "In one, the victim responds to feelings of unmanliness by 'overcompensating', by clinging ever more strongly to traditional terms. Such men, the research suggests, may be dangerous. The coupling of an abused boy's unresolved hurt mixed with a grown man's power produces a volatile compound. In the other outcome of the crisis in masculinity, the men, rather than moving into shamed feelings of inadequacy, question the traditional terms of masculinity itself. Instead of raising the bridge, they divert the river. Having found themselves 'unmanned' these men rewrite the criteria for manhood.

"The violence that abused boys absorb into their being acts like a storage battery, charged with the contempt and shamelessness of the boy's abuser. The harsh child also takes in the general force of contempt for the 'feminine' that is rampant in our culture at large. The discharge of that stored contempt may be a danger to both the boy and to others. In study after study, traumatized boys must come to grips with their trauma, either on their own or with help, if they are not to become abusive fathers" (Walsh, 1997, p. 235-236).

Mr. Walsh made an interesting treatment suggestion to one of his clients: that he carry photographs of his children, who love and count on him. This brief pause and interruption of thought may prevent the man from making a mistake. If he feels himself becoming very angry in a situation, he should look at the picture. The limbic brain's pattern is briefly diverted. I regard that hatred of the "feminine" as a displaced fear in some men: I may weaken in that way. I feel weak.

Tell The Truth/Society Toward Women

Life seems to be cruder than it has been in the past. The honesty and freedom we have had has often led to crassness. This definitely reflects in the sexual arena.

Some people who hold deep anger with women (bad early limbic experience) feel less able to publicly express this anger. The advent of feminism has made this socially unacceptable and even illegal in many venues. There is a kind of backlash that is seen in graphics and the jokes of many comedians. At times, feminism has been foolishly "politically correct, " adding to the backlash. There is also a kind of "Balkanization" of the populace as well. We see groups more eager to "set upon" one another. Each group can make a convincing cognitive argument on why it is a victim. Again, we are seeing people who have had very difficult and unresolved early limbic system experiences.

Tell the Truth/Living in the New Millenium

Back in the 1950's sociologist Paul Goodman was talking about the limbic damage people suffered and inadequate ways of coping with it by the society at large: "Psychologically the picture is more dubious. There is little frustration but there is little satisfaction. General bafflement and insecurity of individuals in the too-big society destroy self-confidence and initiative, and without these there cannot be active enjoyment. Sports and entertainments are passive; the choices on the mass-market are passive; people make nothing for themselves and do nothing for themselves. The quantity of sexuality is increasingly great and approaching adequacy, but the de-sensitization is extreme. It used to be felt that science and technology and reform in mores would bring in an age of happiness. This hope is disappointed; everywhere people are disappointed. Even so far, then, there is evident a reason to smash things, to destroy not this or that part of the system (e.g. the upper class), but the whole system en bloc; for it offers no promise, but only more of the same. And considered more deeply, we have here the condition almost specific for the excitement of primary masochism; continual stimulation and only partial release of tension" (Goodman, 1977, p. 91).

Goodman notes that we are seldom allowed to take decisive action or do our best or even to use our best judgment. The task itself is not valued until it is valued by some "superior." Spontaneity and our instincts are viewed as dangerous and suspect, but we are supposed to be very creative and freely sexual. Wilhelm Reich frequently stressed the anxiety the culture creates for us must release its tension in destruction in order to again feel free.

Good cognitive psychologists have been looking at how the society as a whole affects the individual and his family and what our expectations do to us: "Societies perpetuate these illusions to help the culture-not to help the individual. When the culture teaches that a person will be happier when they reach a particular standard of success, what it really means is that the culture will be more viable; these standards are created to make up for what the society lacks to make it politically or economically strong, making personal happiness quite irrelevant. Thus early America, in need of more citizens, honored the woman who held to the traditional values of home and family, but it was doubtful whether the pioneer woman with 10 children was happy with no freedom, no leisure time, no novelty, a minimum of adult interaction and constant health problems. Likewise, young American men emulating the 19th century Horatio Alger type may have found it hard to be happy working 18 hours a day, seven days a week, just to make another million.

"Human happiness requires far more than fulfilling some cultural prescription for success. We want safety and a feeling of security; we wish to be cared for and to belong; we seek novelty, change and new stimulation; and perhaps most importantly, we want purpose and meaning. Society's petty success goals, like owning the most expensive car or having the whitest teeth, the biggest biceps, or the silkiest hair, are absurd in comparison. Full human happiness is approached by satisfying all our diverse needs, not simply by surrendering to society's fashionable decrees.

"Every culture has created an image of the ideal male, and our society too has its own orthodoxy. Our prototype male is supposed to competently master all aspects of his environment. He should master the physical world by repairing cars, dishwashers, and overrunning toilets with ease, and assembling bikes using only the instruction sheets. He should master the world or finance by driving in expensive cars, affording luxurious houses, and giving his wife fur coats and jewelry. He should master other people by dominating conversations with his quiet grasp of facts and logic. He should be able to defend his mate and offspring from thugs, bullies, and licentious males lusting after the females under his care. He must especially show his power over other males by never being outdone in an argument or humiliated in an athletic contest.

"But simple mastery is not enough. The 'real man' should accomplish all of this while maintaining an impenetrable exterior and 'make my day' elan. Expressing emotions is despicable, so heaven help the man who feels them. Real men have complete control over themselves. These emotions don't even exist for them" (McMullin, 1986, p. 50-51).

McMullin says these demands cause men to feel their genes are suspect if they don't "measure up." The demands impede a man's ability to be close to others, and especially all other males are to be seen as rivals. Men risk collapse as they attempt to adhere to these false standards. McMullin says we have succeeded in spite of our weaknesses, and these weaknesses are simply part of being human.

Tell the Truth/Ethics

Telling the truth must carry through to all aspects of our aspects of our lives. We are not going to feel good, whatever techniques or medications we are using, if we continuously violate the rights and spirits of others. Our culture has become very ethically sloppy, so much so that it seems the prevailing ethos is: do whatever. Just don't get caught. And know that if you do, we will hang you out to dry to cover for our collective guilt.

I believe, deep in our hearts, we all really do know what's right and wrong. The problem is, we like to skip a number of important interim questions which would help us to decide to do, or not do, something. We need to be able to look in the mirror and say to ourselves, this is the plan, I'm doing _____, and not flinch. We need to be able to face our mates or our parents, or our great Aunt Mary from New England and stand behind our plan. If they wouldn't go for our justifications, we don't either, actually. How would our plan fare years later, under the questioning of flinty-eyed attorneys from the top firms in the nation. Would we want our actions printed in the newspapers? Do we want them in our obituaries later for our children and grandchild to save, and God forbid, to have to explain? If what we are doing for sexual pleasure, for limbic system comfort, or for money, does not stand up to this very simple group of questions, there is a problem with the plan.

The Buddha talked a great deal about "right livlihood", in which we serve the planet and do not harm others in pursuit of own gain.

We are frequently seeing people in treatment who do not feel well and happy. In talking with them we discover they are PRESENTLY engaged in wicked or cruel anti-social acts. You cannot feel well if you are violating other people, at home or on your job.

Philosophers like Kierkegaard say we get identity and self-esteem from commitment. We need spiritually and emotionally to declare I am with this person and not that one. I stand for this, but am against that. It carries risk but helps us set goals and realize through mastery of life who we are. We are timid about commitment because life gives no hard guarantees the choice will work out: If I waste my youth on him, will he be kind to me? Will he be a good breadwinner? Will he stay healthy? Will she remain attractive and attentive?

We are caught between nothingness and existential anxiety. Yet we need to choose. We need a type of boundary to respond to. We would not generally sit down to write a novel without an outline. This book is about this, but not about that. It cannot, after all, be about "everything."

Dr. Bernie Siegel is famous for his healing work and he has been an important force in the mind and body again being considered together. Siegel quoted a wonderful motto from the U.S. Marines:
"Tell the truth.
Do your best no matter how trivial the task.
Choose the difficult right over the easy wrong.
Look out for the group before you look out for yourself.
Don't whine or make excuses.

Judge others by their actions and not by their race or other characteristics." (Seigel, 1998, p. 40)

Elie Weisel said our consciences correctly direct our attention to times we did not serve our best interests. That is its purpose, after all, and this is a good thing. He noted, however, that after many times of not doing the right thing, a person can override his conscience. If such a person wants to feel well, to heal, however, he is going to have to begin to tell the truth.

M. Scott Peck has also said we must use discipline to escape suffering. He suggested telling the truth and delaying gratification and being responsible will help us feel the happiness life can hold. The more materialistic the culture, the more frequently achievement is defined only by possessions. The most ferocious the soldier, the more likely he will win for the country. These illusions help the culture itself, but not the individual. These values do not necessarily lead to any personal happiness.

References

Blanton, B. (1991). Telling the Truth. Stanley, VA: Sparrow Hawk Publications.

Branden, N. (1994). Six Pillars of Self-Esteem. New York: Bantam Books.

Canada, G. (1998, February 13). Cherries for My Grandma. The New York Times.
(page A-19).

Goodman, P. (1977). Nature Heals. New York: Free Life Editions.

Janov, A. (1970). Primal Therapy. New York: Putnam.& Sons.

McMullin, R. (1986). Handbook of Cognitive Therapy Techniques. New York: W.W. Norton and Company.

Patent, A. (1984). You Can Have It All. Piermont, NY: Money Mastery Publishing.

Rodegast, P. & Stanton, J. (1985). Emmanuel's Book. New York: Bantam Books.

Siegel, B. (1998). Prescription for Living. New York: Harper Collins.

Walsh, N. (1997). Conversations with God. Charlottesville, VA: Hampton Roads.

CHAPTER NINE: TREATMENT: HOW TO DO IT

We must lower the valence of emotional pain in key individuals in a family if they are ever to work successfully together.

Assemble the family members. I will usually "hear them out" one time in session. This technique works well in marital therapy as well. Listen to the complaints and figure out who is saying what and why. Remember that behind every complaint is: "What about me?"

Diagnosing a case can be compared to a beautiful and very elaborate 1, 000 piece puzzle. In the mental mystery, you assemble pieces and group pieces until you can determine what is appearing before you. Is it a past trauma? A contextual trauma from the original family? Has some discrete trauma occurred to one or more family members? We are creating a clear picture, our diagnosis, just like we create the picture in the jigsaw puzzle, one piece at a time. In the jigsaw puzzle we will finally see a deer, a group of bushes. The more large pieces we can assemble, the more likely we will begin to be able to understand what people and thinking and doing. They may not know themselves what they are really thinking. A good clinician will help the client push past all of his social "postures" and determine what his core beliefs are. What are people thinking and doing that is not serving them? What is causing their discomfort? Like the puzzle, the answers are by no means sitting on the surface for the therapist to pick up. What is really happening can be very subtle, and can be very tricky. The ego has many hiding places and can be quite cunning. In some ways, it doesn't matter what the actual complaints are. We are being told people don't feel comfortable in their worlds. The client may not be honest with us; he may not know what is really happening. But all mental health issues really only tell us: this person does not feel comfortable in his world. All family members are really expressing: my needs are not being met, whatever they are saying with their mouths.

We then treat all family members SEPARATELY, once we have done the initial group session. There is NO value in watching limbic brains run around in the mental squirrel cage we all live in. Sessions that simply tell the story again and again can actually re-traumatize clients and discourage them. They will be more likely to quit therapy altogether. We never want to continuously air the same quarrels without resolution. This, of course, is the reason couples hate marital therapy. Additionally, we run the risk of shaming exposure of deep, embarrassing needs without offering the hope of satisfying them. Having a need AT ALL is embarrassing in our culture, much less having it be publicly seen as not being met.

Health must come from WITHOUT the current thinking system. The "from without" can be through EMDR, a religious experience, affirmations, personal mastery, or interpersonal gestalt experiences. A number of good techniques will be elucidated in this section.

Once family members have calmed, usually after five or six affective sessions, we reassemble them for improved negotiation.

Help clients to use compassion with the self and others. If we could do better, we would be. However grotesquely it may be manifesting in the behavior, given the level of understanding the person has at the time, given the condition of the limbic system of the person, he is doing the very best he can. I recognize this "best" can be quite repugnant at times.

Of course there are magnificent examples of use of powerful force of will, and these are important. Great ability lies latent in all of us. But generally we see people living out their programming. Near the end of his life, someone asked spiritual teacher Ken Keyes if you can trust other people. Keyes replied that you can trust people to behave as they've been programmed to behave.

Keyes had an excellent way of thinking about core beliefs. A belief is like a huge iceberg, most of it unseen beneath the water (the unconscious aspects). In therapy, we chip away at this monstrous block of ice, seemingly to no effect. We chip and chip, trying to rid ourselves of beliefs that hold us back. Finally one day we can get lucky and hit an air pocket in the ice block. It will split, separate and sink, no longer causing danger. What becomes left is much more manageable. Ultimately the whole block of negativity may sink for us.

Even when I see a seriously mentally ill person I try to remember thoughts are mental habits. And, like all habits, can be difficult to change. Yet habits CAN change. When we have a person or family in treatment we always picture them as completely well - their very best selves.

It is work to change a mental habit and I never want my staff to indicate anything else to a client. I sometimes tell people in my private work: "I'm not going to work any harder on your life than you do. Why should I?" There is a kind of mental inertia that keeps habits going, even to our detriment. Clients need to be "pushed."

It's practically possible to drop an imaginary "grid" over a client. This "grid" is steps needed for healing. If the right steps are taken, and the client can extend some measure of trust and willingness, a healing can occur every time. There are rules of health for the mind, just as there are for the body. It's important to have all of the basic underpinnings of health; everything is important. The Buddha said that to have a good life all we need to be is be attentive. Buddhism seems to westerners to be an easy, non-judgmental religion, but in fact, being attentive means being attentive to everything in life. It's actually a large demand of responsibility. To have a healing, we must be attentive to many "underpinnings" of health.

The high level of discouragement we see plays out in many unfortunate ways. We see individuals in treatment of all ages with the sad belief system that says: No one is worth the consistent trouble, even myself. Many failures in the mental health system result from the simple lack of consistent effort.

Again, we see the parallel to physical health. A person can usually ignore some things for a time. Ignore your family life? There will be a high cost. Again, we see the parallel to physical health. All aspects of your life must be kept in balance. As in physical health, psychological issues must be approached before things get too serious. It seems there is a "tipping" point where it is difficult to remediate a situation.

Denial

Denial is a mass activity in our country at this writing. We hope against hope, against all common sense, that something untended will resolve itself to our benefit. The problem builds. An additional problem becomes the fury the individual feels when the denial "game plan" comes crashing to the ground. The individual feels cheated, unfairly thwarted. It was just the universe moving forward, following its inexorable rules, as it always does, always has. The thwarting was not personal.

Whatever we avoid and deny grows larger in our lives. The Indian mystics advise: what you think about expands. The avoidance itself creates a strong mental bond. Because of the mental energy we are expending to avoid something, a strong relationship with it is created. When we fear something, we become much more involved with it. Nor can we simply put it out of our minds by sheer force of will. This is similar to the gag: "Don't think of pink elephants." Of course we are at once thinking of pink elephants, even though we haven't thought of them in years.

The old EST training, which was a kind of motivational seminar, used to say: "There's no one outside of you." This puts the cause of problems squarely into the individual's consciousness where it does belong. This comes as "bad news" to many. But it does give us some power to work with. We can stop laying on the railroad tracks waiting for the train. We were never really tied to the track after all.

It takes character to live a good life. We must be able to consistently, without discouragement, apply our principles. Treatment people need to help our clients take responsibility and realize what their part in problems has been. You cannot rid yourself of the problem until you can admit you have it.

The great Dr. Abraham Maslow said we are always growing toward health, or that, at least, there is that potential. We human beings do fit into the rest of nature and are subject to its forces, for growth or entropy. We are always using "The Force." It is always with us.

Assessment

As stated, all cases in any treatment must begin with a good assessment.

Dr. Michael D. Abruzzese of the Institute for Cognitive and Behavioral Psychology, Inc. in Massachusetts, stresses the importance of a good assessment in working with children. He feels strongly that several data points: parents, teachers, siblings, the child himself, may give a more accurate picture of the child's strengths and needs. Diverse data points will also help track improvement in problem areas more accurately. I see no reason not to transfer any of these ideas to treatment of adults.

The child can heal emotional damage and move forward. We were simply not built to always be out of control. Nature does not operate this way, and we do fit squarely into the rest of nature.

Abrussese recommends asking a child point blank: What are you usually thinking about during the day?

When discussing problematical behavior, it's important for the clinician to know the onset timing of the behavior. Was the child two years of age? Or sixteen? Onset information is helpful with adults as well. With both children and adults try to line up the onset of behavior with biographical information.

To find out what a child's understanding is, the clinician can ask the child to name the emotions he can think of. Sometimes the last emotions named are what the child is usually feeling. We have a chart of faces and corresponding emotions in our office. We have seen adults who cannot name what they feel, even with the expressive cartoon face on the chart assisting.

To look for negative cognitions about the self with the child, the clinician can as: When _____ happens, what do you think about yourself? The child does not have to answer. The thoughts are now in his thinking system. He is beginning to link them to emotions; the processing needed has begun. DO NOT press the reluctant client. We clinicians frequently exacerbate shame rather than relieving it. Only much later in treatment, once we have the client's trust, can we suggest feelings.

We can ask: When is the last time you felt relaxed? Does sleeping relax you?

The way the child is treating other kids can tell us how he is treating himself. Clinicians can ask a child what names he is calling himself in his head. Find out how the child does with relatives and other playmates.

Always find out how parents discipline a child.

Be alert for children or adults who feel they are the "victim." "I've gotten a really raw deal in my life" is a difficult cognition to "unseat." Being the victim has a delicious quality to it and gives away responsibility quite nicely.

Other assessment questions could include:
Has the person tried to take reasonable positive action?
Can he negotiate and compromise with others?
Does the client have any future plans?
Does the client feel well enough to embark on self-improvement protocols?

These are all "markers" to help the clinician assess the degree of damage the client has suffered. Any positive efforts, of course, are good signs. It shows motivation on the part of the client.

CHAPTER TEN: AFFECTIVE TREATMENTS

Meditation

Introduction

Meditation is a wonderful clinical tool. My team uses meditation with hypnotherapy, guided muscle relaxation, and music, which can, and do, reach into the limbic system.

We seldom see a patient who feels a sense of pride in himself. Meditations can begin to work with that lack of pride. It's helpful that embarrassing concepts can be raised for the client without forcing him to respond or comment. Men and adolescent boys in particular are much more able to tolerate a less shaming approach such as meditation.

The clinician can narrate the meditation using a background of music. They can be recorded on cassettes for repeated home use by the client. The trick to this type of affirmation is the repetition, like physical muscle building. It's not that any affirmation per se is so "magical." It helps to set a regular time of day to use a meditation tape; it makes it more likely the client will do it.

John Bradshaw's HOMECOMING has a number of good meditation exercises. They can be used in the same way. If a person is using these exercises and he begins to feel excessively sad or upset, he should return to only relaxations and do the exercises with his clinician's assistance.

Clients using meditations can "cut" the length of time in treatment and move forward much more rapidly. I sometimes appeal to them to do so and thereby "save their wallets, " cutting time in therapy.

With people who feel altogether too humble, more humble than a human being actually is, I will sometimes invoke the idea of some higher power. Something is running your body, something greater than yourself healed that cut. You personally did not know how to assemble the cells. Did you know how to re-grow that skin? Something digested your breakfast for you. Did you intellectually know how to break down your oatmeal to do that? Or is there something "great" operating in you? That is pretty amazing.

We need to teach our kids and ourselves: there is nothing better than what you already are: a human being, uniquely crafted and developed. Each person is a totally unique set of DNA, physical characteristics, personality. No one can better be "Johnny" better than "Johnny." Not the clinician. It's a meaningless proposition. Again, my favorite maxim: Tell the Truth. It "clears the deck" for something new. We are unique, even if we may not be fond of what we think we "are". We are not replicated anywhere on the planet, not at this, or any other, time.

The Meditations

<u>Paul Solomon</u>

By far the most powerful meditation I've ever used is based on an idea from the Rev. Paul Solomon, but most gestalt therapies have a variation on these themes as well.

Imagine being in the most magnificent place on earth. Imagine sitting in the environment. You control the only access to this area and you are all alone, but you are not at all lonely. What would you see? Would the sky be overcast or clear? Are there any animals nearby? If you reached out and touched something with your hands in this most beautiful place, what would it be? Would it be soft grass? Or would you be touching tiny pebbles in a shallow creek? Perhaps you would be running your fingers through smooth sand? What fragrances are in the air? Perhaps you are smelling the salt spray smell of a beautiful ocean area. Is it the smell of fresh pine needles in a forest? Perhaps you are smelling the smell of freshly cut grass? Make it as real as you can. What colors do you perceive? The place can be a real place or a made-up place.

And now, you see, slowly walking toward you, a figure. It is not threatening in any way. The figure is moving very slowly and you feel yourself to be protected in this magical place. As the person gets closer, you realize that this figure is the figure of your mother, looking as you normally think of her looking. She is silent, and stops right before you. Communicate with her. Communicate in a way that is safer than the ways we have here on earth. In this magical place, speak to her heart to heart. She will not become angry or hurt as people often do on earth. Look into her eyes and tell her what it has been like to be her child. What has been good? What has she shared with you that you value? What has been very difficult? What do you wish had never happened at all? If she has an explanation for you, listen to it. Do you have any reply to her? If you feel "o.k." enough about her, hug her and let her go.

Let her go completely and go back to the beautiful place. (Go back through environmental cues.)

(Repeat meditation with father, and lastly self.)

You looking at you calls your attention to this fact: this may be the most difficult relationship of all. Imagine your hurt self, the one who embarrasses you; the one who does all the bad things. Imagine your strong self. You, looking at you, what do you think of yourself? What do you love about yourself? What do you hate? Is there any way you can be more in support of yourself? Can you imagine that you need your support most of all? Why are you reluctant to give this support? Is there any way you can promise yourself more care and support in the future? Can you imagine sending yourself love for the journey ahead? Let yourself go, and go back to the beautiful place.

(Repeat environmental cues.)

Bring clients slowly out of this meditation and all meditations. I do not force clients to discuss this information if they are new to me. The affective processing has begun; the clinician can be assured the limbic system is engaged. This is a very powerful meditation. It can be used repeatedly to good effect. If clients are willing to discuss some of their insights from the meditation, it gleans valuable information for the therapist. If they are not, at least scan the body for reaction. Is the person's stomach tight? Are muscles affected? Is there a lump or sadness in the throat? Did a headache appear? At what point in the meditation did any body systems become activated?

Most clients will share this type of information even if they are reluctant to tell much else.

Ron Smotherman

When people are very "fed up" with others in their environment, this Ron Smotherman meditation can be both fun and insightful. We live in a social world. We do need others.

"Go with me on an imaginary trip. This trip begins in Nothing, which as you know is nowhere. You are actually going to make this trip alone although I will be your guide. You are going to come out of nothing and enter a world where there are no living creatures, not even plants. You are going to take a living form much like the one you have now, except that you will be totally alone. Now that I have guided you to this world devoid of life, I am going to leave you and you will forget who brought you. You will not only not be with anyone, you will not even remember being with anyone. Now, sit back and experience what life is like on this planet.

"If you are very conscious, you will be able to perceive on this forsaken planet you have no idea that you exist. There is absolutely no one and no thing to validate you, or even tell you that you are there. You are going to live out your life in this condition. The parts of your body seem as irrelevant as the rock around you. Your sex drive is a total mystery to you. You have no idea of what vision is, although your eyes see some things. You are confused by the few sounds you hear. You have no idea of the purpose of anything you have. If you had a language to think in (which you don't), you might think that life is not worth living. But you don't even know you are alive, so that never occurs to you. Your body changes as the years pass and eventually you die, not knowing that you lived. Your only relationships were at the absolute physical level where, when you bumped a rock, it moved. I have painted a picture of no relationship to give you a sense of what relationship is all about. Relationship is about experiencing your Self. But there is a hook in the system: you cannot directly experience your Self because you are stuck with your physicality. Therefore, you will have to experience and express your relationship through your machine" (Smotherman, 1980, p. 127).

The Black Trunk Exercise

A common Eastern meditative practice involves having the client place all of what he regards as his attributes in a container. After they are in the container, the client can realize that what he really is, is ineffable, ethereal and ephemeral. A soul.

The therapist can use a standard muscle relaxation or a guided relaxation exercise to prepare a client for the Black Trunk Exercise.

Ask the client to imagine a large black trunk. It can be embellished with a taffeta lining, brass nailheads, etc., depending on the clinician's imagination. The client can then systematically place all the things that he "thinks" are "him" into the trunk.

The person's name, the job, the family, the mate, the appearance, the color of eyes, the sex, all accomplishments, all things disliked and liked, can be placed in the trunk. The sound of the voice, the job, everything the client has ever owned, his car, his house, his favorite outfit, all can be placed in the box.

The client is then asked to realize that he is none of the things he has always identified as "him". He is much more. He has the power to place the things, and the power that stands outside of the trunk. He is an ineffable force that cannot be limited by any judgement or situation.

Memory Exercises

Memory exercises can both relax and reaffirm to the client that there is more to his life than just depression and suffering. If we have been suffering we become inclined to think that is all there is for us. The clinician can use music or any relaxation to create the setting for the actual meditation. I often use a Thought Field Therapy to strengthen the treatment.

Ask the client to recall various experiences:

Remember a time you felt handsome…
Recall a time you solved a serious problem…
Recall a time you were afraid and were not sure things would be "o.k." and they were.
Recall a time someone else put trust in you.
Remember a time when you stuck to your position.
Recall a time when someone treated you with respect.
Recall a time when you felt a friend did love you.
Remember a time when you felt very able.
Remember a time when you hugged someone else and felt close to another human being.
Remember a time when you surrendered and it was a good thing.
Remember a time when you listened to the ocean or a river or a creek.
Recall a time when you felt very capable.
Remember a time when you were petting an animal and it was relaxing and good.
Recall a time when you didn't care about the opinion of society.
Remember looking at a beautiful landscape or sunset.
Recall a time when you "fell for" someone else.
Remember a time you "made up" with someone you had fought with.
Recall a time when you "goofed up" and enjoyed it
Remember a time when someone was very honest with you and you felt close to him.

Remind your client that if he or she doesn't have a memory for the particular incident. It's "o.k." Just wait for the next one. I sometimes say "We're not doing anything, we're just hanging out. There are no expectations."

I also remind a client that the very fact that he has recalled even one of these positive memories shows that life is a mosaic; there's more to life than simply suffering and pain. It's much more involved than that; in even the hardest life, there are some good times, some things that bring joy. People very much tend to "filter out" these thoughts and become involved in their sad stories. An occasional jolt into the positive is a good thing. The more in love with their stories, the more people will fight the positive memories. That tells the clinician the client is imagining a fairly important "payoff" for maintaining his story.

The Wrong-Hand Letter

John Bradshaw has a good technique in his book, Homecoming. He suggests writing a letter to an important individual in the life of the client with the non-dominant hand. I suggest that the client put some music on and allow the mood to flow freely. Promise the self that the letter will never be sent, no one will know, no one will be given a chance to become angry or to feel hurt because of anything said in the letter. Using the non-dominant hand allows the feelings to come to the surface and to some degree, prevents the intellectual, logical self from interfering too much with the process. Often feelings we have never allowed to come to consciousness begin to surface. Just telling the truth about them begins the healing process. We can deal with anything we can tell the truth about. If the process becomes too painful, or raises too many difficult feelings, rather than becoming too upset, it would be better for the client to do the exercise with a clinician at hand.

Special Uses of Guided Relaxation

Many clients, especially some males, may not even recognize what they are feeling. Some of them have been using suppression for so long, they have dampened their ability to genuinely feel and identify thoughts. If a client has developed some trust in the clinician, it is possible to tell him what he is feeling. If we are wrong, clients will jump to correct us. When we are correct, and it's not hard as we share such commonality of desires in our humanness, we can spare the client the shame of saying out loud what he needs and what he has been hurt by. It calls the issue to consciousness for the client and addresses it in an honest and genuine manner. The processing so desperately needed has begun for the client.

Eye Movement Desensitization and Reprocessing (EMDR)

I like to think I found EMDR because I needed the tool so badly. I was working for a Domestic Abuse and Rape Crisis Center. I used standard exposure techniques and guided relaxations with hypnotherapy and was able to help clients gain some relief.

However, what was occurring was that the clients were suffering more and more severe traumas and the trauma was deeply encoded in the consciousnesses. A middle-aged waitress had a striking plight. She had been savagely raped at gunpoint along Route 80 one night while her car was stalled. She had not slept well since and could barely work. She had a teenaged daughter who depended upon her. Her husband could not comfort her and she was anxious and angry most of the day.

She revealed that her workplace diner was frequented by State Troopers. She saw a gun on one of the troopers two or three times per week. Each sight of a gun caused the horrible night along Route 80 to come flooding back to her. She knew it was not a rational issue, but the emotional residue rose inexorably when she saw a gun.

Hypnotherapy and guided relaxation gave her limited relief. EMDR could have prevented this woman from feeling immobilized two or three times per week. I saw her at least twice per week and worked to implant the suggestions that the rape was in the past and she was presently safe, but the sightings of a gun seemed to "undo" whatever I was doing.

EMDR is a treatment which accelerates the treatment of depression, guilt, anger, phobias, and self-esteem issues. It is especially effective with discrete trauma. These issues can be present or past issues.

It is not hypnosis and the client is fully conscious at all times. It is a distraction therapy, and the work of the eye movements seems to help keep the client's rational mind busy enough to break into his dysfunctional, habitual thinking patterns.

The treatment was originated by Francine Shapiro, Ph.D. It has been used in California and some Veteran's Administration hospitals since 1988. The ATF has used the treatment and it has increasingly seen applications in Critical Care Incident Work. EMDR clinicians helped victims and workers at the Oklahoma City bombing site. No negative side effects have been noted but there is a less clear memory of negative events following treatment. There is a relatively rapid decrease of symptoms.

The statement of a police officer at a Critical Care Incident Treatment seminar I attended was memorable. He had been badly traumatized by seeing the death of an infant in a traffic accident. A young father, he watched in astonishment as the baby's severed head rolled by him. He admitted his instinct was foolish, but he chased the head with the idea of replacing it onto the child's shoulders to "repair" the situation. He was haunted by this image for years and was very distraught he had not been able to save the child. He gained instant relief when treated with EMDR.

Shapiro postulated that the processing of situations moves them into appropriate storage in the declarative memory and reduces the pathological reactions to them: "To reiterate, our working hypothesis is that the symptoms of PTSD are caused by disturbing information stored in the nervous system. This information is stored in the same form in which it was initially experienced, because the information-processing system has, for some reason, been blocked. Even years later, the rape victim may still experience the fear, see the rapist's face, and feel his hands on her body, just as if the assault were happening all over again. In effect, the information is frozen in time, isolated in its own neuro network, and stored in its originally disturbing state-specific form. Because its biological/chemical/electrical receptors are unable to appropriately facilitate transmission between neural structures, the neuro network in which the old information is stored is effectively isolated. No new learning can take place because subsequent therapeutic information cannot link associatively with it. Therefore, when thoughts of the incident arise, they are still connected to all the negative attributions of the original event. The results of years of talk therapy, of reading self-help books, and of experiencing counterexamples are also stored, but they reside in their own neuro network. It is in part the disparity between this theraputic information and the dysfunctionally stored information that impels the client into the therapist's office for treatment and has him say, 'I shouldn't be this way'" (Shapiro, 1995, p. 40).

In a sense, very extremely emotional events have been "gated off" by the brain and are causing an overreaction to present day situations, especially any situation which reminds the person of the original event in any way. In order for new thoughts about the trauma to enter and help calm the client, the "gated off" area must be reached. Dr. John Omaha says when we just talk to clients about traumas, it's like clicking on the wrong folder on the desktop. We're just not in the right area; we need access to the limbic system. I talk to clients about unfreezing frozen memories, making them turn into "water", and washing them out. The basic memory of the event will remain, but the emotional valance can be greatly lowered, giving enormous relief.

Francine Shapiro postulates that EMDR helps by activating the information processing system. The dual focus is key; a present stimuli is linked to a past traumatic experience. The eye movements themselves serve as a distraction to the pressure felt, helping the person to move the information. The trauma was frozen in time and was caught in its own neurological network. It was stored, but in a disturbing state-specific structure. The person's self healing structures have been thrown off balance. As the person ages, more and more neurons are co-opted into the imbalance. I tell clients that, cognitively, they have accumulated more and more evidence it is a dangerous and arbitrary world.

Thoughts and beliefs formed during trauma but about the self, are causing present day maladaptive behavior. The treatment must address the original trauma or incident. Current triggers of these memories (like the guns for my client) which cause maladaptive behavior must be found and linked to the past stresses. The clinician then will help the client install a more adaptive current response (i.e. I am safe now) which then helps the client increase his feelings of self-efficacy. Emotion may not disappear, but it will seem more appropriate to the situation, and not have the very large amplitude which can the frighten others and the client himself.

It is very interesting how memory is stored. EMDR can give the clinician a look inside the person's thought processing system. He can tell us what he decided about the event, even though that thought may not be usually conscious for the person. The muscles of the body and even olfactory senses are involved in traumatic memory. I did a session with a nice teenager who was caught in a violent parental marital fight. She remembered she had been making a cake with her dad when her mother burst into the room. The parents became involved in a serious altercation. In reprocessing the event the client vividly smelled the butter cream frosting of that cake from long ago.

Another client recalled being raped outdoors many years ago in the fall. She smelled the burning leaves she had smelled then, and remembered the smooth feel of the cardboard the rapist put her on. She realized suddenly she had always hated the fall. Now she knew why.

Another teenaged had an irrational dislike of the sight of digital numbers. In session she remembered her father raping her in her bedroom. On her shelf she had a clock with blue digital numbers on it. She used to pretend she had gone up into that clock and wasn't present on the bed during the rapes.

During the affective treatments, clinicians will check with clients and note body responses. Headaches, sick or fluttery stomachs are very common. Tight muscles, especially in shoulders and necks, and forearms are common. The neck and shoulders almost "gear up" for blows they expect to be rained upon them. The forearms and hands may be tight because originally the person wanted to take action, and the movement was truncated or ineffective. Events can "sicken" us, and we even say in our language, "I couldn't stomach it." Throats can be tight or hold "lumps". We are seeing sadness, or perhaps a truncated statement the client was not able to make at the time. Interesting work has been done with headaches. Some are cognitive "caps": I didn't want to think about it." Headaches at the base of the skull may indicate the client tried to block his energy from coming from his body, up the spine as energy, and then to the thinking brain to be evaluated. "Heartaches" can be literal during sessions and people sometimes find a racing heart or difficult breathing accompanies bad memories. It is speculation, but I had to laugh at the skill of a young doctor I had in session. He was a man with a fierce force of will, and when he had unpleasant thoughts about being treated badly as a youngest brother he "pushed" pain all the way down into his feet, and felt pressure in both feet-as far away from his "cognitive cap" as he could. He didn't want to think about it. The ways in which we cope with stress are a varied as human personalities, yet there are some common themes and similarities.

Neuroscience has found that intense fear experience DOESN'T go to the thinking part of the brain first. The body may race the heart without the mind immediately being aware of WHY this might be happening. We find ourselves dealing with archival stimuli which has set very disturbing responses in motion. Therapists have joked that it is well the brain developed in this manner; if a sabre-toothed tiger wanted to eat you, you needed a very rapid response. You could not hang around and intellectually process the situation.

Trauma presents many problems for the sufferer. We need to believe the world is reasonable. We need to see that it can be socially modulated and that we have a chance at protecting ourselves. The trauma victim needs to renegotiate his personal safety and he must have some safe attachments.

Some clinicians say the body keeps score. There will be physical and mental results if the person/organism has been seriously violated. Because they have a form of hyperarousal, trauma victims tend to shut down. Remaining on a semi-permanent "red alert" is exhausting. They fear the intensity of their emotions and the emotions also remind them of their former failure to affect the outcome of their lives.

In laboratory experiments, repeatedly shocked animals have lower serotonin levels. They will also show a stress induced analgesia. The serotonin reuptake drugs are very popular for human beings at this writing.

Traumatized children will show problems in their ability to competently narrate events. A chaotic narrative style will cause problems with writing, reading and communication skills. All of these are skills that are vital for successful school learning. It's as though, following trauma, the person is so busy attending to safety, to "make sure it never happens again" that all of his others skills are diminished.

Dr. Bessel van der Kolk feels that traumatic experience must be put into time for the client. The event had a beginning, the client now is in the middle, and the event will eventually end. One of the best cognitive ideas that can be "installed" into a treatment session is that the event IS in the past. It is not happening now. The gated material must be accessed for this evaluation to help the client, however.

Secondary stressors following a trauma can re-traumatize a client. A woman in treatment described being in an ambulance with a person who had died. The ambulance was very bloody. Sometimes the life is so altered the person will have to move. Sometimes a large part of the problems is that peers and family members know what has transpired and it has altered their relationship to the client.

It's helpful to let clients know, when using EMDR, that they may be affected following the sessions. It's a bit like having a strong emotion "ripped out" suddenly. The clients may continue the processing during the week, and find themselves seeing images of the event, remembering details of the event, having experiences in the body, and perhaps dreaming of the situation. These are all ways of moving the event along, continuing the needed reprocessing. Following a practice EMDR session in a training, I suddenly had an image of my grandfather's ugly embossed grey rug. I had not been in his home since I was eleven or twelve years old.

Uses During Assessment

I will sometimes use bi-lateral "tapping" even during assessments, when a client is forced to tell me a difficult story that involves grief or loss. The assessment can actually serve as a treatment as well, lowering the valence of the event for the client. The treatment is diagnostic as well. It the client continues to dissociate back into the trauma it will be readily apparent in the affective treatments. The clinician can get a good gauge of the amount of recovery the client has done, and what is needed.

Other Affective Treatments

Tapas Fleming in California has done excellent work with the body: "When a trauma happens, a person's response is usually, 'that's too much for me.' The implication of that inner statement is, 'I'll get to it later, file it away, and face it when I can, when it isn't too life threatening.' But we seem to put off forever something that we don't want to deal with now, and the trauma that we put off if still with us. We have simply put time and distance between us and the event, but not the experience itself. The experience is still on hold, and the illusion has been created in our minds that it is in the 'past', and that we are in control of our lives. However, in fact, the stronger we keep it in the so-called past, the more strongly we are connected to it. And the more experiences we hold off like this, the more narrow and limited our lives become.

"A trauma occurs when life becomes unbearable and you tell it, 'No.'. Or variations on the theme which could include: 'Hold it right there. This is too much for me.' 'If this happens I won't survive.' This is not necessarily a conscious choice. It is a natural response to your life in the moment. This response sets up patterns of mental, emotional, and physical behavior and health. A blockage, or energy stagnation has just been put in place and your life has been impacted. It seems like a good idea at the time, but you lose the ability of distinguishing the difference between a truly life-threatening event and an event that merely has certain aspects that resemble the original traumatic event. It is as if life were a flowing stream, and at one point, out of fear you roll a boulder into it to try to dam the flow in order to keep a traumatic event from happening to you. The water, of course, simply flows around the boulder, but in your life-in your body, mind, emotions-there is a blockage that wasn't there before" (Fleming, 1996, p. 5-28).

Thought Field Work

Dr. Roger Callahan introduced his Applied Kinesiology in January of 1985. He uses the body's energy meridians in the way acupuncture uses them. Blocks in energy flow can be relieved by applying pressure to certain points in the body's energy meridians. Fear IS energy, and it creates powerful blocks to healthy body energy flow. Dr Callahan uses rhythmic tapping on locations on the client's body rather than actually puncturing the body. He gives instruction for some eye movements at times. He uses some cognitive work. He is using the kinesiology to help the client deal with phobias, various forms of self-sabotage, and fears of all types. He also treats anger and sadness with the tapping treatment. Like EMDR, immediate results are obtained in sessions. Some relief is achieved in the very first session.

Dr. Callahan says his new Thought Field Therapy "bypasses cognition." At the beginning of a session, a client is asked to picture a disturbing situation and to rate it according to how much pain it causes him. There is, however, very little, if any, actual cognitive restructuring. Dr. Callahan is relying on the body's energy systems and the treatment is entirely safe.

Post Traumatic Stress Disorder in the Civil War was called "Soldier's Heart." In World War I it was called shell shock. In World War II it was called traumatic neurosis and battle fatigue.

Uncontrollable stress has a serious biological impact. A person cannot be violated again and again with impunity. Neuroscience is indicating the brain itself can be physically damaged by trauma and contextual stress. I believe in years to come we will indicate contextual stress, that day-in and day-out verbal abuse we normal give to each other in our relationships will be viewed as very traumatizing, perhaps more so than even some discrete traumas because of the lengthy duration of a relationship.

Apparently victims form an "intention" to avoid the pressure in severe traumas. People decide to refuse awareness to escape bad moments.

The new therapies are successful in trying to interest and engage the brain. It can be difficult, and often the cognitive systems in the person will resist new ideas.

The brain is attracted to what seems new and different. This is why we see flashy graphics used in advertising so often. This makes video games and their odd sets and characters attractive to the mind. The brain looks to what it knows already. The brain is trying to create a consistent pattern.

Because of the tendency to "pattern", we often mistake one written word for another that we are more familiar with. The spelling may be very similar, perhaps only differing by one letter. The brain will "complete" the word by assuming what it is seeing: the more familiar word. This explains how thinking becomes habitual with individuals. They fear the same things, decide the same decisions, etc.

Interrupting a thinking pattern must be done in the moment. Good gestalt work will call the pattern vividly to the client's attention in the moment, giving a change to think differently. Many of these gestalt moments occur using EMDR or Thought Field Therapies. The client has an opportunity to see belief patterns in a new light. These therapies are effective because they do reactivate a stressful pattern and bring it right into the present, giving an opportunity to now think about it in a different way.

Conclusion

Affective treatments work wonders. However, one of the greatest problems we encounter in Family-Based work is the need to use affective treatments, which do render the client temporarily more vulnerable. Ideally, this type of treatment is done in the presence of a secure attached relationship. Many families have been "squabbling" for years and are very cruel to each other behind closed doors. (Even more worrisome are the people who will be rude to each other in front of the therapist.) It is problematical to "open up" painful areas when a client lives in an unsafe atmosphere. For at least the first four or five weeks of EMDR treatment, the client may be unusually labile and sensitive. We must weigh these issues out on a regular basis. For the same reasons, it is difficult to use EMDR in a residential or a prison setting, although the client could clearly benefit from the work.

Bessel van der Kolk has addressed the need to reestablish social connections and a sense of personal efficacy in the trauma patient. He explains why some clients seem to have "shut down" feelings: "Again, because in people with PTSD so many roads seem to lead to traumatic associations, much of their efforts are geared toward NOT feeling and thinking. They have given up on believing that they can figure out how to regulate their internal states" (van der Kolk, 1996, p. 427).

There may be depression or upset in a person he/she had to agree to surrender in a dangerous experience that could not reasonably be evaded. At times, people will harbor an unrealistic "big screen" image of bravado that is actually seldom seen in daily life. This type of bravado might have actually cost the client's life in severely dangerous moments. Men are particularly prone to making these demands upon themselves. A shame can follow: "I am not a man like Stallone is."

In general, we have found that good affective work, especially EMDR and Thought Field Therapy, moves the client forward very dramatically and far more rapidly than months of any other type of therapy can accomplish. These affective therapies seem to open the "right folder" on the desktop as therapist John Omaha tells us.

Once an individual family member calms, he is more likely to succeed in treatment, which then brings in a partner and children. The freedom to change, to shift ideas, to move forward, is determined by what blocks the client has. What are his belief structures saying? What personal and religious principles does he have? Does he have character and determination, at least enough to do the work? What is the strength of his character? All of these answers will become clear using affective treatment.

Post Traumatic Stress Disorder

PTSD was a landmark recognition by the legal and psychiatric community that an external event can serve as the direct cause of a mental weakness. The diagnosis creates difficulty for the legal community as a person has lost neither his contact with reality nor his appreciation of right vs. wrong. In order to work in a insanity defense the person should be in a full-blown dissociative state or a flashback state. It has long been clear to psychologists that a person can be very substantially shaped by how he is treated by others.

The affective techniques are very good for helping the client uncover what his core beliefs are, and these anxieties are always related to issues of safety. Reportedly, Albert Einstein's final inquiry was "Is the Universe safe?", a salient question for all of us. We feel angry at a world that doesn't seem to support and love us.

In a certain sense, all mental illness means the person, for some reason, does not feel safe in his world. He then picks one of myriad ways of withdrawing. The withdrawing can become habit, and can be difficult to break. He becomes "stuck" with his defense mechanism. It is the job of the clinician to help the client identify and admit what "scared" him, help him see he did at least survive the threat (perhaps not elegantly, but he did survive it) and build up his sense of power to negotiate a reasonable and supportive world for himself.

Each of us is quite unique. We are a tiny piece of some larger, unknown consciousness. We need to feel the value in ourselves and others. We need to stop violating the life force in ourselves and others, including animals. We need to begin to respect our common life force. Then life will begin to feel more navigable.

Nancy Marshall, M.A.

References

Fleming, T. (1996). <u>Reduce Traumatic Stress in Minutes.</u> Torrance, CA: Self-published.
Shapiro, F. (1995). <u>EMDR.</u> New York: Guilford Press.
Smotherman, R. (1980). <u>Winning Through Enlightenment.</u> San Francisco: Context Publications.
van der Kolk, B. et. al. (1996). <u>Traumatic Stress.</u> New York: Guilford Press.

CHAPTER ELEVEN – GESTALT WORK

Gestalt therapy refers to affective work which is accomplished "in the moment" with the client. It is highly experiential in style. Interpersonal interactions take place and the client is moved to abrupt and new realizations as a result of these interactions: "When the interpretation reaches its mark, it will tie together one's consciousness with the new data from the unconscious and one will experience the unity which makes him whole again" (Polster & Polster, 1973, p. 46).

Basically, the skillful interaction in a gestalt therapy session helps the client to suddenly see things in a different manner. Fritz Perls called it the "Aha" moment. The gestalt therapist must watch carefully for his moment, and move in rapidly, causing the client to question his long-held beliefs.

I Should

"I Should" is the old bugaboo for all of us. It is always the person's most critical voice. The Gestalt therapists would ask the client, "Yes, but what do you WANT to do?" Gestalt therapists can be very directive and will usually insist that the client answer the question, and rapidly, without a great deal of defensive pondering. Examination of the "I Shoulds" will help uncover resentments clients have been harboring but may not want to openly claim.

We have found resentment to be the major block in family relationships. All of us have done unfortunate things with loved ones; it's so very vital to be able to let go of them and move forward: "There is another great advantage to using resentment in therapy, in growth. Behind every resentment there are demands. So now I want all of you to talk directly to the same person as before, and express the demands behind the resentments. The demand is the only real form of communication. Get your demands into the open. Do this also as self-expression: formulate your demands in the form of an imperative, a command.

"Now to back to the resentments you expressed toward the person. Remember EXACTLY what you resented. Scratch out the word RESENT and say APPRECIATE. Appreciate what you resented before. Then go on to tell this person what else you appreciate in them. Again try to get the feeling that you actually communicate with them.

"If you have had difficulties in communication with somebody, look for your resentments. Resentments are among the worst possible unfinished situations-unfinished gestalts" (Perls, 1972, p. 52).

Feeling Thwarted

If a client expresses feeling thwarted or cheated in a situation, use an affective meditative exercise with the client. Have him reach deeply into the negativity and anger over the situation. Make it very dramatic for the client. Have him imagine he will NEVER RECEIVE SATISFACTION in the situation. It will never resolve. Ask the client what negative feelings and fears are coming up in response to the "never."

Help the client understand the fear that is "lurking" beneath the suffering, usually: "I'm not good, " or, "I'm so not good, I'll be abandoned."

Assertion Skills

Most clients need better assertion skills. They need to be able to directly refuse a pressure. This ability will truncate negativity and avert the need to be dishonest and "sneaky, " which damages self-esteem and destroys character development. Good affective work will automatically lead to better assertion skills. As the fears calm, the person's already existing self-preservation ability will appear. This happens automatically, and the client will not need "assertion skills training." In order to be assertive, a client must believe he can do it. Always we are working with the belief systems. That means calming the deeper fears.

Gestalt therapists have moved clients' fears in interesting ways. Clients can try out assertion skills in interpersonal gestalt role-playing. The next time the person needs to assert himself in real life will be slightly easier because of the gestalt practice. Each time assertion is mastered after that, the client will begin to feel more powerful. Limbic system patterns are changing.

In interpersonal work, it can always be revealing to ask someone: what's making you talk to him in that teeny, tiny voice?

"I may ask a client to talk to imaginary forces within himself, to address people in his life, to sing, or dance, to jump or change his voice, to pound pillows, to assure attitudes of gruffness, hardness, softness, anger, sweetness, sentimentality" (Zinker, 1977, p. 124).

With his intense focus on the client's operant belief structure, and his creativity, the gestalt therapy can assist a client in suddenly seeing everything in a new light, in the moment: "Let us say I ask a shy woman who feels inferior in her femininity to walk across the room as if she were a very sensual person as a way of changing one's self perception" (Zinker, 1977, p. 132).

By doing it, the client becomes more the behavior. By acting in the moment even though it feels very awkward (and it will), the client shifts his belief structure: I can do this. It feels odd, but the earth didn't stop on its axis. I can do it.

We are actually helping the client to develop character. The blockages people feel are illusions, but they can feel very solid and very true to the person at the time. Good gestalt work challenges the client in the moment, and he moves beyond what he had formerly thought himself to be capable of.

A favorite exercise of mine was taken from Gestalt therapy. It works wonders with a resistant client. It was successful for me with groups of angry adolescent males, a very historically difficult clientele. Take an ordinary rubber ball, a plain one, at least seven inches in diameter. Inscribe on it in permanent marker a number of sentence completions:

"Mom, I want to tell you…"

"Dad, you never would…"

"A perfect life for me is…".

The ball is then tossed from client to client spontaneously. Wherever the client's right index finger rests, he must answer that question. I also add several Off-the-Hook spaces, so clients can feel they are getting away with something if they do not have to answer. I also usually play myself, and if there is a co-therapist, have him play, to equalize the playing field and build rapport with clients. Teenagers love it when I have to answer question after question and they keep getting "No Question". If people seem very reticent or upset I "let them off the hook." There is never any value in deeply shaming anyone in front of the group.

This exercise can open up ideas, can assist you in your assessment of the problems the person faces, and can create a sense of fun. It works well with a client alone in session as well. There is something oddly powerful about calling out a response in a gestalt session; it really catches the mind's attention. The limbic system has been "hooked."

References

Perls, F. (1972). <u>Gestalt Therapy Verbatim.</u> New York: Bantam Books.

Polster, E. & Polster, M. (1973). <u>Gestalt Therapy Integrated.</u> New York: Vintage Books.

Zinker, J. (1977). <u>Creative Process in Gestalt Therapy.</u> New York: Vintage Books.

CHAPTER TWELWE: TEACH THE CLIENT

As stated, one of the chief causes of failure in treatment is that people do not try long enough and hard enough. There are numerous "pieces" to a complete healing for any individual. It is foolish to not consider all of the elements needed.   Clinicians routinely overlook physical health in their patients when treating for mental disorders. We have found again and again that we can do a good job treating contextual or discrete trauma in a child, only to send him to a school where people shame and "corner him, " causing explosive, self-sabotaging behavior. People need to learn a whole new way of talking to themselves in their own minds. We all harbor disastrous habits in the self-talk area, and this, after all, is the "climate" in which an individual's brain lives. People need to do their healing, and then be able to move out into the world and gain a bit of mastery somewhere, and a bit of love somewhere. All of these things become the vital "underpinnings" to the healing. This Chapter will discuss numerous treatment modalities and ideas.   A good Family-Based treatment person should be conversant with these ideas, as well as the affective therapies. Missing any of the underpinnings can limit or destroy the healing.

Supportive Self Talk

We believe the talk going through our own heads. Our strong self is trying to help, but he can be something of a slave driver: I have to do this job.   Weak _____(person's own name) can't be trusted. He is a slob. He needs to be pushed and controlled. I have to "improve him."

We need to tell that scared self we do understand. We want him to do better. But, we need to learn to speak to him more gently so he doesn't shut down. We need to tell that scared self we want to make life easier for him; we know he feels it's been hard. He needs to be encouraged, not accused. If we can be honest, we'll notice the scared self is very blaming and nasty and critical toward others as well. We see the return of normal human empathy immediately when we are able to calm this scared self.

The scared self inside of us all needs to be told he has our support and love "no matter what". We need to tell that self it won't matter if he doesn't radically change. That scared self could be happier and succeed more easily with some changes, but he is fine just as he is. Only then can we successfully work for improvement in behavior.

I tell my clinicians that to continuously "pound" on clients who already feel sad will leave us alone in the treatment session. The client will "disappear, " leaving us holding a wad of "wet Kleenex." A discouraged person needs encouragement, and lots of it.

These are problems of the human condition. Again, we are talking about degree, and degree only. All of us have learned to speak to ourselves in unsupportive ways. It is endemic in every culture. All of the world's great religions attempt to help us learn to value ourselves and care for ourselves. We clinicians are not so very different from our clients. Being a human being is a humbling experience. All of us win some and lose some.

One of the best ways to work with self-talk, and the cost cannot be beaten, is with written affirmations. We have our clients write a statement they do not believe, i.e. "I am a good person." This should be written daily five or ten times for several months. It should be written by the non-dominant hand as this affects the way the brain receives it, and is an effort to bypass judgements. A slow but steady application will help chip away at a negative belief.

It is very important to not blame the mind for it's negativity. In a tricky "Catch-22" way, criticizing the mind for criticizing only adds to the problem. Jesus was a master psychologist, and this is what he meant by "Resist not evil." The Indian mystic, J. Krishnamurti said to just notice what the mind is doing. Just notice, with no judgement or criticism. I have told clients to even look in the mirror and pat their heads, telling the mind, "Calm down, I see what you are doing. Just relax. We'll be o.k."

Always look carefully at self-talk. Typical unsupportive self-talk for all of us looks like:

No one loves or cares for me.

I can't offer much, especially when compared to others.

I'll look like a fool if I speak up.

I deserve it, and I will be punished in the future.

What will it mean if my partner has a good time out without me?

What do other people think of me?

Nothing I do matters.

Nothing ever works out for me.

It's proper for me to be responsible and grim. It proves I'm very adult.

What bad things are going to happen next in my life?

Supportive self-talk takes discipline: "Self discipline is a habit. It consists of installing new self-talk. Telling myself 'There will be enough' is helpful. Asking questions like 'How many times have I starved or gone without my basic needs in the last few years?' helps me even more. I may even laugh when I ask such a question. When I answer it, I realize how fear distorts my thinking. Self-monitoring asks one to develop good habits, to be virtuous" (Bradshaw, 1992, p. 271).

John Bradshaw is aware of how "catching" dark thoughts can be: "At my treatment center...we often say: 'YOU EITHER PASS IT BACK OR YOU PASS IT ON'" (Bradshaw, 1992, p. 190).

We frequently berate ourselves for having been naïve in a situation, but we need to re-frame the failure as needing to increase our powers of DISCERNMENT-no big deal.

Beginning Individuation/Where Self-Talk Begins

The "terrible twos" and other young child behavior that we regard so problematical are really the beginnings of the child starting to see that sometimes his interests and those of his parents are going to necessarily be at odds.

If parents continuously "shut down" the silly grandiose dreams and outlandish behavior of young children, the constant suppressing can create sadness and later, depression. Healthy young children have a feeling of their own power, and of themselves as important heroes. Especially if the parents lack self-esteem, this egotism can be embarrassing to parents. We often do what our parents did to us. Let your child embarrass you now and then. Big deal.

We can scare children so they won't follow their dreams. That will protect them from the embarrassment of trying for something and not achieving it. It will also guarantee them of a disappointing and unrealized future. The child will soon learn to suppress himself (the critical parent voice some therapies refer to). He has internalized the "child abuse" of not believing in himself and his dreams.

A child, even an awkward child is a wonderful thing. There's nothing more wonderful or more engaging than a growing and developing person. He can certainly develop skills and become much more able, and do things better, but he'll never be better, because right now he is a remarkable being. Most people realize that we love young children because they are a little wild and uninhibited, qualities we may miss in ourselves. Rev. Paul Solomon elucidated this very well for young parents.

Neither the critical strong side of the person, nor the weak, degenerate side of a person is "real". These are roles constructed by the mind. These constructions are ever changing, plastic. In one moment a man may be weak and dishonest. Actions a moment later can belie this and he may find himself rising to whatever occasions he must rise to. Part of what the world's great religions prescribe for us to deal with these ego images that scare us so is simply to stay in the moment.

I like Eckhart Tolle's book, THE POWER OF NOW. We are not what we were yesterday. We are our actions today. We can move toward tomorrow with more confidence if we ignore the ego constructs. The inherent self is wonderful. He may have flaws, may have done bad things in the past; he probably will do bad things in the future. But he is a completely unique being never before seen on earth. He can be more successful at meeting his needs than he is, but he will never be any "better" than he is right now because there is only the one "him". There is no way to compare and find lack.

The Rev. Paul Solomon taught me about the life force that binds us all inexorably together. Even those who don't believe in the powerful binding force are using its energy at all times, even when they are doing something "bad" or violating another.

Negativity

When bombarded with negative experiences and people, it is very important to not continue to meditate on them. This is, regrettably, quite difficult to do. The Eastern gurus have told us what you think about expands. In that same way, take the action you are able to take with a problem, and then put it out of your mind. If you need to, attempt to fill your mind with something else with as much force as you can. To meditate on the negativity is to increase it, to let it totally control you. You are then giving your enemy a victory over your consciousness. He is in control of you and how you feel.

Use of Affirmation Tapes

Like the written affirmations, affirmation tapes repeated daily can help shift belief systems. A cassette tape of personal affirmations is easy to make at home. Any standard hypnotherapy book can suggest good relaxation exercises and visualizations. I like to use some type of music or nature sound effects tape in the background. Suggestions can then be introduced. A suggestion must ALWAYS be framed in the positive. It should be what the client does NOT believe. "I am safe." "It's safe for me to be in a close relationship." "I can earn the money I need and want." The daily repetition is the key. It's certainly not that any one listening is so helpful.

Louise Hay in California has a very good affirmation tape available. It is called "Overcoming Fears." Her telephone number is 1-800-654-5126. She addresses work issues, travel anxieties, relationship fears and many others.

Sentence Completion

Sentence completion is very useful for assessments. Clients will reveal their philosophies of life on many existential issues. I did an internship in a drug and alcohol rehabilitation hospital for teenagers and we used a sentence completion test as part of the intake. For some reason people feel less inhibited in writing something, and the kids were often surprisingly frank. We need to have some understanding of a client's life philosophy to help move his cognitions into more supportive thoughts. Some examples:
I feel empty when.
It hurt me that.
Life would not be worth living if it weren't for.
I make myself feel more alive by.I'm different, in that.
A good life is.
I feel proud of myself when.
I'm ashamed when I.

This is clearly the same principle as used in the Gestalt ball. They key is to answer the questions rapidly, before the socialized rational mind gives its answer. These types of sentences can be used in session as well, even without the ball. I have sometimes tossed an available stuffed animal, or something or that sort, which was available in my office, to the client, insisting he answer the question immediately upon catching the toy.

Learn to Have Fun

Self-care is a vital part of feeling healthy and happy. Many people have so lost the ability that it must be assigned. I myself have even used my date book to schedule in hearing music, seeing a friend. The demanding rational mind, called the critical parent in us in some therapies, is very rigid and not inclined to do anything but drive us, and drive us hard. There is always a reason why one can't take any time off or spend a few dollars on the self. Some clinicians say if we don't do some things enjoyed with our money, we will associate money in a negative way, and be less able to earn money.

People should make an effort to find healthy interests that feel supportive to them. Any number of creative hobbies are available, and music, because it reaches the limbic system in a very intense way, is always helpful. The dissonant, angry music so extant at this time should be avoided as it simply adds to a jittery nervous system's problems. I also do not think most television is helpful. So little of it has any uplifting qualities. I do not like the reality shows and real-life shows that seem to make fun of others and encourage our negative projections onto other people. It does us no good to continuously view other people living their lives in a shabby manner. It feeds a negative sense of superiority in us, but only temporarily.

One year when I was unemployed in New York I checked out all of the Shakespeare plays and followed the recordings in text, developing an understanding of the plays. Of course he was a master psychologist, making the plays quite interesting to me. The world is full of many interesting things to study: history, animals, all sorts of other sciences, etc. Life really is short. Why waste precious time not engaging the mind?

Art Therapy

Art therapy is a highly engaging therapy and there are many good books in the field. It can help someone who feels too damaged to talk, isn't sure of what words to use, and is very shy. People who are afraid to speak will often draw or paint or use clay or sand.

One of my clinicians was good with art therapy. In an earlier assessment of two parents and their three children we got quite a laugh. We had concerns about the parents and they seemed to be very passive aggressive with each other. One boy drew his parents in shark-infested waters with their arms up helplessly. There were sharks all around. There was a small island and on it was a tree. The three kids were high up in the tree, looking down at the scene. The therapist asked the artist if the parents were saying anything. Oh, yes. Help, help. He asked whether the kids were saying anything. Yeah.

What were the kids saying? The kids were saying "Ha, ha, ha." That pretty much did our assessment for us.

Use of Music

It is generally quite helpful to play or listen to music. The great classics, work by Mozart and Beethoven and such, would be best. There are good artists working contemporarily, but anything angry should be avoided. The steady drone of the television set is omnipresent in homes, but people would feel more happy if they were listening to music.

The Physical Body

I can't understand how people can think they will have good mental health if they neglect or mistreat their bodies. Therapist Carol Bloom used to talk about overeating when we're sad as about as sensible as putting "french fries on a cut." It's the wrong balm, at the wrong time. It just won't heal emotional pain. The most one can hope for is a temporary "logey" feeling, the results from overeating. Exercise is essential for the lymph system as it has no central pump of its own. It must rely on motion of large muscles to help the lymph flow and clean the body of toxins. Exercise can help tame personal demons. Moving energy through the body is very useful. The use of acupuncture can move blocked energy and change emotional status. I personally use acupuncture for mental health care. Very often a person can express emotion more freely following an acupuncture treatment. Acupuncture is especially useful when the person simply feels "drained" and may not be sure what he or she is even thinking about, what has been the source of distress. I recommend acupuncture for maintenance care. Extra "B" vitamins, those complexes that contain Choline and Inositol will help any anxious person. The essential fatty fish oils in vogue for heart care are also very good for the nervous system. Diet expert Dr. Robert Atkins is presently being vindicated by the medical establishment after all of these years, and the carbohydrates and sugars are what is bad for our bodies. Anyone interested should also read books on Syndrome X, which discusses pancreas failures so extant in the culture. People want to sweeten a life that feels "sour" with sugar, but do so at a high cost to health.

The body also needs sleep, and this is obvious, but often ignored. When I am under great pressure this is something I have forced myself to do, to good effect. Like all "children, " I hate to get up, but want to stay awake late at night watching an old movie or reading. I have to make myself go to bed. Plain Melatonin from the health store is a safe sleep aid.

The Princeton Brain Bio-Center is doing incredibly good work on mental health with vitamin and supplement therapy. To approach mental health in this manner requires determination and dedication as the diet restrictions can seem severe. Most people have some undiagnosed food allergies, and ignoring this weakens the organism significantly. I personally would insist that anyone I loved be treated in the orthomolecular method. Some doctors are having wonderful success with autistic children using the fatty fish oils as a supplement for them.

It seems foolish to not do all you can in your environment, especially as there are factors that will never be in our control. Why not control those things that you can?

Some other people have found new mental stability by checking for environmental allergies and clearing the environment. There are good specialists all over the country working in these areas.

Help the client begin to notice and understand the body during the treatment period. Encourage the client to understand the body and the clues it hold for understanding the mind. Take note of its changes. Have the client note the tiny new cut on his leg. When did that happen? And the bruise on his arm. What birthmarks does he have and where? Have they changed at all over the years? Has his body changed at all over the years? During periods of large change, what was he going through in his life? What was he thinking about? When he's tense or afraid, does his body feel differently? How does his body feel when he is happy?

Many clients can be taught to learn when the body is initially becoming angry or afraid. By learning this, emotional action can be taken before the anger or fear becomes too extreme, and thus, is harder to deal with. Sometimes the very best one can do is simply to move his body-to another area.

We commonly see people in treatment who only want to "boss" their bodies around, and want to generally ignore there is anything below the neck to contend with. People need to learn to really inhabit their bodies and not always be trying to escape from them. Massage, karate, all types of training that remind us we are in a body that needs care are helpful. The body can become an ally, and it is there at all times, acting as a feedback unit for our emotions.

Use of Dreams

Some skill in dream analysis is useful for any therapist. There are many good books on dream analysis available on the market. The clinician should read a number of them and most individuals will find them quite approachable as well. A dream can be a "report card" on how the treatment is going. It is generally regarded that when the person begins to take action in his dreams, rather than passively accepting, say, a monster chasing him, he is beginning to feel stronger. His ego is developing and he feels more powerful. The therapy is taking hold.

Fantasy Story

I liked an idea I saw in a conflict resolution course. The team created stories of various adventures. They left the names blank, and the child's own name could be individually filled in, making him the hero in his own "myth." This can work subtly to help a child think of himself in a new way. Comic drawings can be used to illustrate this exercise.

Goals

Help clients to separate their goals. What are really important needs, goals and dreams? Is he delaying taking important classes that could move him forward because he "needs" a new couch? Determine which needs are really closest to his heart. Set the most important priorities. List them and look at them on paper. Sometimes writing the goals gives an additional clarity.

A very old friend of mine, a poor Italian boy from the Bronx, wanted badly to be a doctor. His parents were no longer alive, and if they had been they wouldn't have had any money to help him anyway. He stumbled around Manhattan for a decade, upset he didn't have a rich family to send him to medical school. He did take a night job in the Medical Examiner's office that gave him the feeling of being near the medical field.

In a sweep of boldness, after a romantic loss, Bert went on a quiz show and won a substantial amount of money. He opened the back section of the Sunday New York Times and scanned the medical schools. The fall semester had already started before he got his money. People had been advising him medical schools only like the very young students, right out of colleges. He would never be admitted. He called a school in Mexico on a Sunday. To his, and our, surprise, the Dean of the school answered the telephone. He let Bert begin at once. After a semester, following failures at the University of Texas medical school, he was given the chance to take one of the openings in Texas. He transferred. To survive his residency, back in New York, Bert lived in our friend's theatre. He had no bathroom of his own, no kitchen, no privacy of any sort. The place was always bustling. Bert lived there simply with only a Mr. Coffee machine and his hotplate for years. Today, he has a successful medical practice in the northeastern United States, a beautiful wife, and a young son. "Lifestyle" was not as important to him as his dreams.

The old EST training used to say we could have almost anything if we really INTENDED to have it, and the degree and power of the intention was what made the difference in having and not having.

Responsibility

Handle small duties well, especially if all you have are small, boring duties. Large responsibilities will flow. Do with all of your might what is right in front of you. Keep good care of your car, your home, your clothing etc. Think of yourself as deserving the best care a person can get. So what if right now the care is only coming from yourself? Who better knows what you really need? Return calls, pay bills, do everything to the best of your ability. Don't "hold back" energy for the time you really need it. Do your very best right now, every day. The energy will renew itself.

There is a mental "feedback loop" that comes from MASTERY of the small details in life. It's training for a greater mastery. Mastery is a good source of self-esteem. Begin where you are. Master it. This, of course, has been a principle in Eastern religions for centuries.

Medication

It has been noted that we Americans are a practical people, liking practical solutions to problems. However, sometimes a short cut is not a good thing. It's important to remember that when we talk about medicating a client's behavior, we are talking about putting medication into his entire body, not just his brain.

Medicine is profitable. It is heavily marketed in glamorous ways to doctors, hospitals, and increasingly the public at large. The general population is exposed to pharmaceutical advertising as never before.

I am against the "chemical straight jacket, " especially for young people. Doctor's office time must be spent on kids and their parents. The clinician must listen to the patient and the family. Young people will often not know how to, or even that they should, describe their reactions to medications.

Mental health involves the ability to negotiate the world. It involves the ability to help loved ones understand I do want to be loved like this, I don't like that. Employment and all sorts of consumer issues involve the ability to negotiate. A child will not build these skills without practice. And practice involves facing moments of stress, weathering them, and building interpersonal mastery. All of this is more difficult to do when heavily medicated. It also does not become any easier as time goes by and we avoid the skill-building. A person needs "antennae" to read emotional responses from others. He needs to build courage and character under stress. None of these tasks becomes easier with age.

For children and adults, medication can give the false promise to the client that he will not have to face areas in life that are difficult and require character. It will not "shelve" forever the need to face issues in his life. The appropriate use of most psychotropic medication is to temporarily aid the client as he steps forward to heal, and later, to face challenges in his life: "Patients and clinicians interviewed about the adjustment to well-being describe a range of reactions. 'Once you leave depression, you're back in the world where people have problems and have to make compromises and decisions and have too much to do, ' said one patient" (Fox, 1998, p. 3, Section 4)

Mental health requires feeling confident that we can negotiate with others and have our needs met: "The idea of having a 'disease' can be appealing when we lack confidence in our capacity to overcome our problems. If depression is a disease, then we take encouragement from turning to our doctors. And we can stop blaming ourselves so much. All this is very understandable and very human, but it's not necessarily the correct or best way to view human suffering and its relief" (Breggin, 1994, p. 186-187).

Used wisely, medication can act as a "bridge" while the client strengthens and builds skill in therapy.

A fascinating article in The New York Times stated that British psychiatrists are reluctant to prescribe medication for hyperactivity unless it is quite severe. The use of Ritalin-like medications has remained stable in England, but pharmaceutical companies in America have increased production 250 percent since 1991. (Angier, 1994, p. 1, Section 4)

Dr. Edgar Hallowell, a child psychiatrist at Harvard has noted that boyish behavior is suspect these days because of Americans' fears of crime and all aggression. Whole groups of people who act with what the population might regard as too full of vitality or aggression are under enormous suspicion. The unwholesome mix of fear must now include fear of terrorists.

The orthomolecular work done in Princeton, New Jersey is of great interest to me. Doctors are using GABA and food supplements of all sorts. A good vitamin B complex is helpful to the nervous system, as are the fish oils readily available in any health store. Self-control is developed by the child's central nervous system. The metabolic system and its health is a factor. If we want good emotional functioning we ignore the body at our peril.

Dr. Peter Breggin has written about medication in a careful manner, and anyone using medication would be well advised to read what he has to say.

The Princeton Brain Bio Center is doing some of the best work extant with nutrition.

PRINCETON BRAIN BIO CENTER
842 State Road
Princeton, New Jersey 08540
609-924-8607

Change Environment

Some changes can be very simple and useful. Simply opening the blinds and flooding a home with light can help. A clean environment creates a context for health. Housework is not something we get up in the morning to do, but keeping a home clean and free of clutter is very helpful to functioning. We have entered homes that were truly amazing in their level of poor care. I recall one home, which was in a nice corner lot with lovely trees, and was shocking on the interior. Geological layers of filth, clothes, newspapers, and one "spongey"

172

layer that concerned us most of all covered every square inch of the floor in every room. It was about seven inches high, so that one was lifted off the ground walking there. Doors were frozen ajar in their positions as the rubble built. Our first move was to purchase several boxes of garbage bags and work with the family to get it all out.

Pictures for the wall, especially anything spiritually uplifting, are a good idea. Almost everyone can afford a can of paint to brighten dingy areas.

Put up family pictures and start to honor the members of the family. Interestingly, it's often easy to tell who is being "scapegoated" in a family. Usually his pictures are fewer, or missing altogether. Bright children's drawings enhance any area.

Spirituality

A person needs some type of belief system. I understand that many people have had hard lives and are angry at God, and don't want to hear about him. Fine. There are other ways to approach spirituality. Creative work of all types is a spiritual thing. Simply looking at nature and its wonders is spiritual. God proves his benevolence by the regularity in nature. Summer always follows spring, year after year, no matter what negative foolishness man is up to. The ocean waves keep coming in. Small animals still play and like to be played with. A garden is a wonderful way to connect to God, as is farming. People do not have to go to a formal church if they do not want to. I do encourage people to read from the various great religions of the world and see what makes sense to them or comforts them in any way. I like to go periodically to a local Buddhist monastery and stay for a few days. It's lovely to be immersed in a place where people are interested in higher values. It always causes me to think a bit differently.

Personal Journal

Many people find healing in keeping a personal journal. They simply diary their thoughts and feelings and impressions of the day.

We can gain insight into what we are thinking in these journals. They can also be helpful through time. Clients should look back at what they thought was so vital, and, or, so terrible last year: something they didn't think they would survive. It's interesting to see how well they actually did with it can build confidence. Remember, we don't have to handle a situation perfectly, we just have to HANDLE it. I do have a caution about the personal journal. It can become one long confabulation: Just sad story, sad story, sad story, cementing negative belief systems. If this is a pattern, the person needs some other types of interventions.

Mary Pipher

I liked Mary Pipher's book, SHELTER OF EACH OTHER. She has had the courage to say to parents they must teach their children they are not the absolute center of the universe. They can survive if their every need is not satisfied immediately. She warns us to not just let the culture "happen" to us. We will be fat, broke, overly medicated etc. So many messages extant are only to help others get into our wallets.

Dr. Pipher also criticizes the cowardly and ubiquitous cynicism we see everywhere in 2004.

Certainly it's hard to change things. It takes courage to declare ourselves. Being too afraid to try helps us lose before we ever even leave the "starting gate."

Encourage The Client

Encourage your client to reassess his life periodically. What is he committing himself to in life at this exact time? Who is he giving love to, receiving love from? Some of the motivational business speakers encourage people to examine these issues daily to keep recommitting to the principles that actually interest us. The world is full of distractions; it is very easy for us to lose our way. "Busyness" does not necessarily at all mean we are moving toward a good goal. It only means we are very busy.

Help your client imagine how dull perfection would be. There would not be any news or events to react to. Life doesn't have to flow perfectly. It won't anyway, so we have no choice but to change what we can and enjoy the adventure of the rest.

In treatment circles of late, plain old force of will have too often been ignored. All of us have untapped inherent strength. Strength will increase as it is used, as well. It is fair and clinically helpful for the clinician to encourage and "push" the client to use his force of will. Hold the client to a high standard, but kindly.

On Managing Our Tempers

John Bradshaw suggests the corny (but still viable) old "Count to Ten, " then trying to think of another response when under pressure. Anything that interrupts our automatic patterns and allows a "space" for a new approach is a benefit. The automatic patterns come straight from our limbic brains, and the response may have too much valence for what is actually occurring, to our detriment.

When we deal with loved ones, or people with who we do not want to sever the relationship, "Count to Ten" can assist us. We often feel proud when we have an especially clever, if cruel, retort to "attack" with. But the price tag on that clever retort may be higher than we would like it to be.

Name It – What Are We Actually Doing?

In good cognitive work we must accurately identify what is going on. Do not allow clients to obfuscate and put a good 'spin" on destructive behavior. The following descriptions of personalities and negative ways of relating to others will be familiar to all of us. Their purpose is always to give "the player" an advantage in interpersonal negotiations.

The Martyr

You can tell the martyr. He is playing to an "empty house." The drama is very sad, and very well rehearsed. It is sometimes accompanied by physical illness, which heightens the pathos. Remind such a person everyone else is busy feeling sorry for himself. They don't really have time to buy a ticket to his show and listen to the sad drama. IF they do listen, it will be for a few seconds, then they will "slough it off" and move on. There's no one in the house. Why run the show? Is the show to prove to parents how much they have failed him? How it's all their fault? They have long since moved on with their lives. He may raise a bit of residual guilt in others, which they feel for a fleeting moment, but will never admit to him. He won't get that satisfaction. Why should a man ruin his whole life like that for some type of inadequate, puny revenge?

Another favorite martyr game is to give and give to another. Ken Keyes used to call it giving a gift you can't afford. After some time, the martyr will turn on the other, furious. He has been taken advantage of.

The Passive Aggressive

This person is very angry. He has a core feeling: "How dare anyone tell me what to do? How dare anyone cross me in this way? I'll get him, even if I have to wait a long time for the opportunity. Don't allow this client to play "nice". Make him admit these motivations. He was squelched as a child and needs revenge. He must come to grips with these motivations to move away from this alienating behavior. His parents told him he was not "ok" and that the world would not accept him. He has been contextually threatened in this demeaning way for years. He needs to tell the truth about it in treatment and not exact revenge in the present day. This will poison the world further for him. A number of drug and alcohol treatment specialists say that all addicts are passive aggressive.

The Obsessive Compulsive

The Obssessive Compulsive is very frightened. Be gentle with criticism of the client; he is already so afraid. He feels errors are bad and they must not be made. The world is unsafe, and he will be further threatened if anyone figures out how unable and flawed he is. He must face this truth and understand emotionally how unrealistic his goal is. All of us are flawed and are learning new things each day. A reasonable effort is all the world needs from us, not perfection. Help the client see he has a right to live, even in his "imperfect" state. He doesn't need to do anything to justify his existence. Here he is. Someone wanted him here. He can safely live.

The Histrionic

This theatrical person is afraid of being abandoned. Please don't leave me. Notice me. I'm interesting. A lot of dramatic things happen around me. Help this person see these fears and come to grips with his demands. Help him to understand too much drama may drive everyone away from him. None of us wants our lives to be a walking hospital to take care of the needs of another. We all want to live our own lives and self-actualize and have companionship. The theatrical histrionic risks scaring us all off.

The Avoidant/Dependent Person

This person wants a stronger person to know that he is helpless. He needs to have it done for him. Don't ask too much of him, world. Help this client to achieve small bits of mastery in work in the field if the structure of the treatment allows this. Gently move him forward and help him feel the positive feedback loop of accomplishment. The feedback loop of success will build courage and self esteem for this client. Like the martyr, he needs to be told his audience is not there. All of us have our own problems. We do not want to devote our lives to tending the problems of one who is "helpless." Interestingly, a great many of the violent partners in domestic violence situation fit this pattern. They are not skillful in building emotional bonds to another and fear they will be quite helpless if the partner leaves. They "up" the aggression to prevent the one they depend on from fleeing.

Columbo

In cognitive work one can "Do a Columbo." Feign a lack of understanding, but explore the client's techniques for survival. Ask him if his way has worked. When did it work? Explore the approaches he takes to life together and move toward conclusions in unison.

Anthony Robbins

The business power motivator Anthony Robbins has clients ask themselves what they have given today. What excites them in life-now, this very day.

The idea of giving is alien to people who feel very wounded and "put upon." It is corny but very true, that one way of making the self feel better is to do for others. A genuine effort on behalf of another can "take you out of yourself" and cause you to feel more calm and happy. We exist in community. Help the client find a balance between a necessary self-involvement and efforts for others. EST was right on target on this as well. They used to say that if you have a problem, a good way of working with it is to take on another, larger problem. The first problem will recede into the background.

How Are We Helping Ourselves?

Most of our behavior is an effort to change the way we feel. We often make frantic "adjustments" with little or no understanding of how they will work. Some choices, like that to become involved with addiction, do have a body of literature to help us think about the choices.

People need to understand that if they don't make a plan for their lifetimes, and decide to drift along like a stick in a rushing river, the world will make a choice for them. And they may not like the choice that is made.

Examine very strongly held beliefs very seriously. Try to determine who taught the person that belief. Was the person really wise? Was this person worth modeling his life after?

Some beliefs seem very hidden from us. Look, then at the behavior. What would a person behaving that way have to be believing? Try to track the belief back through the feeling. What beliefs must the person hold, according to how he is feeling?

Fear of Aggressive Others

If a client explains that ever since he was a child, if anyone yelled at him, he felt terrible. The clinician can try to reframe this for the client. Is everyone yelling at you going to be allowed to make you feel terrible? How about when a crazy person in the street yells at you? Does that make you feel terrible? Or a clown at the circus who is playing to the crowd? Does that make you feel terrible? We need to help people feel secure and refuse to accept assessments of their value from every Tom, Dick, and Harry who walks by. Affective work on the original damage will help these clients greatly. This is contextual trauma.

Forgiveness

It's very difficult to feel healthy when we are constantly focused on past injustices: "Forgiving someone is solid proof of your intent to live your life now, while you have it, and be dead later on, when you are . . . So you are doing the 'forgiving' for you, so that you can get off your grudge and get your life on the road. You see, you have a lot of vital energy tied up in your grudges. By detaching yourself you get all that energy back" (Smotherman, 1980, p. 103-104).

Guilt

In this culture we use guilt as a method of self-improvement. We're hoping to curb negative inclinations in ourselves in the future: "If you feel guilty, what that means is that your are going to do it again . . . Guilt is a currency, which people use to pay for the evil things they do, imagine they do, or simply imagine. Once whatever it is paid for with adequate guilt, you are then ready to do it again . . . The basic foundation of guilt is the fear that you are the person you are afraid you are" (Smotherman, 1980, p. 19-20).

I think you can find pretty much whatever you want to know about life in the vintage Warner Brother cartoons. The late Chuck Jones said all of the animators liked to imagine they were Bugs Bunny: fearless, fair, only attacking when attacked. But what they feared they really were was Daffy Duck: greedy, cowardly, selfish.

Blame

Blame disempowers us. It keeps you lost in the altercation or conflict and makes the feeling of impending doom greater. The best thing you can think is: "This has happened. I don't like it, but here it is anyway. What can I do now?"

Fix-It – All Clients

Don't give a gift you cannot afford. Many times we are only giving to GET. Our mental ledger is counting, brimming with resentments over what we have done for the other. When our resentments increase to a large enough size, the other person will be angrily presented with a huge bill.

Working with the Discouraged Client

The discouraged client only fears trying to do something will only open up the self to new hurts. Why bother?

Try to have the client tell you if he has ever felt good about the self. When was he doing well? Was he ever satisfied with the self? These are always good questions to ask periodically, even recording the answers to later encourage the client. Sentence completion exercises can yield the answers for clients. The Gestalt ball exercise can be very helpful.

Try to help the client see that he is not being "charming" and humble in his hatred of self: "Help the client examine beliefs that have not been useful to him. Originally formed to help a client escape shame in vulnerable years, the thoughts are no longer serving him:
1. The worst thing in life is to fail.
2. If I don't totally win, I fail.
3. Success is an illusion; failure is real.
4. One must in control of everything (self and environment) or one will fail.
5. If I can't do something perfectly, I shouldn't do it at all.
6. I am running out of time to succeed.
7. If I worry about failing, I'll be more likely to succeed.
8. I must have everybody respect and approve of me.

It is easy to see what impossible demands these beliefs create. It is not humanly possible to meet these demands at all times, yet people struggle and strive and become angry at themselves when they cannot meet them" (McMullin, 1986, p. 96-97).

On Unnecessary Worry

"The fear is appropriate to the probability of the danger occurring. If a person is afraid of being hit by a meteor, the fear would be irrational because of the low probability. Some clients are remarkably irrational about low-probability tragedies, while totally oblivious to such higher probability dangers as automobile accidents.

"Being alert about having a 'nervous breakdown' doesn't reduce the probability of having one" (McMullin, 1986, p. 123).

Good, careful, cognitive restructuring can help a client if it is done respectfully.

People engage in compulsive behavior as a way of ordering their world and comforting the frightened self:
"Schema: Unless I engage in this ritual (counting my steps when I walk to my car), I will get into a car wreck.
Probe: Maybe you are using the wrong ritual. Perhaps the correct ritual is not to count. How would you know? How many accidents were you in before you began this ritual?" (McMullin, 1986, p. 129).

I like this suggestion for clients. It can help them feel compassion for the self: "Picture that a young, bright, psychologically healthy person is given over to your care for ten years. You have the power to control his/her environment for this time. Now let us suppose that you had to teach him/her to be as upset as you have been. What would you do? Specifically, how would you get him/her to believe he/she was inferior, sick, stupid, or any of the other beliefs that you have about yourself? And what are the key subcomponents of each of these beliefs that you would have to first teach? How would you teach these subparts?" (McMullin, 1986, p. 216).

Self-Dislike

If a person is holding a negative idea which is limiting him, explore other avenues of thinking with him. Explore the opposing ideas. If he feels stupid, ask him when did he ever feel smart? When was he "handsome" and "successful?"

It can be useful to ferret out areas of achievement and put them on an index card for use later. The person's negative mind will filter achievements out of his past again. The card can remind the client of a time when he did feel able, etc. The card can be posted on a bathroom mirror for the client to look at daily.

On Motivation

I've used certain adjunct books continuously in my practice. I like Barbara Sher's WISHCRAFT very much: "You're only going to live once. YOU MUST HAVE WHAT YOU WANT. So draw up a list of all the things you think you have to do. Then cross out everything you would cross out if you were going to die in six months. And then stop doing. Your house may not run right. Your lifestyle may go through some interesting mutations. But no one is doing to die, no one will get scurvy, no one's teeth will fall out and no one is going to throw you out on the street for not being a Good Woman or a Good Provider . . . "A sudden loss of interest in your goal: it fascinated you in theory, but in reality it's boring, not for you at all (NOTE; Hidden fear will try to trick you into changing your goal whenever it starts getting challenging. That's why so many of us have picked up and dropped so many activities-not because we're dilettantes who can't make up our minds.)" (Sher, 1979, p. 180-199).

She addresses the inertia caused by our fears of discomfort: "Because I happen to believe that missing out on your dreams and never finding out what you're capable of is a hell of a high price to pay for peace" (Sher, 1979, p. 199).

To Aid in Forgiving the Self

Take out pictures of yourself as a small child. Look at the innocent little person you were and realize that child has been through some very difficult experiences. That child has suffered and has made the best adaptation he could at the moment, even if he did bad things. Try to imagine loving and forgiving him and being willing to stand by him as he attempts to grow in character.

Spend more time thinking about and being with people who do love and support you. Think less about the people who do not and cannot support you. If the Indian mystics were correct, and what you think about expands, why put energy into enemies?

Use your sense of humor. Even if you have failed horribly at something, you can write a good "Don't Do It This Way" book. You can be a good bad example. Life goes on.

We often use our minds in a completely habitual, not useful manner, for all of the wonderful thinking capacities we have. A rat who is not reaching the "cheese" in a maze will adapt his technique to gain some cheese. EST pointed out many humans will keep on going down that tunnel which has no cheese, has never had cheese, never will have cheese. Humans will then waste a lifetime telling whoever is foolish enough to listen, there USED TO BE CHEESE IN THAT TUNNNEL. By rights, THERE SHOULD HAVE BEEN CHEESE.

A human mind seems to have developed to replay images of past events that the person thinks will help him survive in the future. Of course, this is essence of Post Traumatic Stress Disorder. The mind that suffered through an automobile accident is convinced there will be another, and a permanent state of "Red Alert" will protect the organism in the future.

EST wisely taught that we either have results, or a lot of excuses why we don't have results. The old EST training used to make a very valid point about worrying and catastrophizing. If you are not experiencing a thing right now, in your life, why worry about it? Many people do have cancer, right now. If you do not, is cancer really that "real" for you? Isn't there enough in the everyday environment to worry about, the things you must attend to? Why add to these day-to-day burdens by meditating on fear? What you think about expands. Some say that meditating on fear helps bring bad experiences into the life. In any case, we often scare ourselves with what ISN'T. And ignore what is.

One of the good things EST did for people was to ask them to challenge their own rational minds. Rather than constantly "salute" pat beliefs, the EST training asked participants to look to their own experience. (Another variation on being in the now.) It doesn't matter what people say about anything if you cannot find validation for it in your own life.

This certainly causes parents difficulty. We ask our children to take our word for so much of life. So often they don't want to. Some common sense safety issues must take precedence in our parenting, but often we could let the child go ahead and experiment and see for himself. At worse he might get wet, muddy, or embarrassed now and then. And he would really remember the lesson.

Much of the culturally honored "worrying" could be averted. We just don't have much earthquake activity in Pennsylvania, where I presently live. How much do I want to worry about it? The river behind my house, which does flood, is not flooding today. Should I worry about it today? Should I use up that psychic energy I could do something else with? If it does flood, I'll have to take action. But it may never flood. However, I'm not stupid. I learned how to shut off the electric power if I need to. If it's really going to flood. The trick is to respond in the moment-to what actually is.

By the same token, I am not going to spend one moment worrying about terrorism. I'm going to live my life was well as I can and as honorably as I can.

Paul Solomon wrote a number of excellent small books that I use frequently in my work.

On reconciling relationships: "They are playing a role in your life, giving you a choice of scripts. Will you choose to play the victim who also strikes out in pain, hoping beyond hope to find some love in a hostile world? Or will you choose the script that recognizes another person's weakness and need for support, extend to them understanding, and find inside of yourself love to support yourself and to extend the same to others. Be for-giving, a person whose life is for-giving. That is, for giving whatever supports life" (Solomon & Haslam, 1986, p. 41).

On handling the self: "Guilt and blame of self for difficulties of life will only lead to more guilt, lack of confidence, ineffectiveness and immobilization" (Solomon & Haslam, 1986, p. 67).

On relating to others: "And yours is the only love you have to give, so shut up and give it . . .You could compare yourself to other people or to storybook heroes and believe that in comparison your fire loses its brilliance. There may be some valid point in such an evaluation. You might be 'naming the name' of some of the limitations that are restricting the expression of your fire. But consider this: those storybook characters are not alive right now in the moment. You are. The only person occupying your body right here, right now, is you, and you can apply your vitality to what is before you. Other people to whom you might compare yourself likewise are not available right there in your place. Only you can contribute your liveliness. Even the old you who has done better or the future you who should be able to shine more brightly are not present in the moment. And the moment is the only time that the fire needs to be expressed" (Solomon & Haslam, 1986, p. 67-74).

Anxiety

A standard question often asked of clients in Neuro-Linguistic Programming therapy is: "What must I be sure of?" This question is a quick way to assess fears and find out what is causing the client's daily reactions.

References

Angier, N. (1994, July 24). The Debilitating Malady Called Boyhood. The New York Times. Page 1, Section 4

Bradshaw, J. (1992). Creating Love. New York: Bantam Books.

Breggin, P. (1994). Talking Back to Prozac. New York: St. Martin's Press.

Fox, M. (1998, October 4). With Prozac, The Rose Garden Had Hidden Thorns. The New York Times. Page Section 4, Page 3.

McMullin, R. 1986). Handbook of Cognitive Therapy. New York: W. W. Norton and Co.

Sher, B. (1979). Wishcraft. New York: Ballantine Books.

Smotherman, R. (1980). Winning Through Enlightenment. San Francisco: Context Publications.

Solomon, Paul. (1986). Restaging Your Life in Three Acts. Timberville, VA: The Master's Press.

CHAPTER THIRTEEN: WORKING WITH CHILDREN

Working With Young Children

Paul Solomon was the best guide to raising young children that I ever encountered: "Children often get our attention by misbehaving. We all do that, at least a bit. We see this in adult relationships as well. During the arguments, they traded fully of their energies, thus each provoked the other. Unconsciously, they each were thinking, "If I can't get your attention through supportive actions, I'll get it by misbehaving . . . We use our name, money, power, and accomplishments to justify our existence and feel alright about ourselves. We do not have to use any of these to justify our existence. Our existence is already justified by the fact that we are here . . . A child living in a particularly disciplined household will find some way of maintaining control.   It may be through temper tantrums, withdrawal, or even severe illness. In its positive sense, the need to maintain control is the innate awareness that I am responsible for my life." (Solomon & de Pont, 1985, p. 30-32).

Solomon suggested ways in which parents could use comparison in a positive way: "I look at you and see a quality I admire. I want to be the best that I can be, so I observe your strength, your beauty, your poise, your confidence. I want that, not because you have it, but because I have seen something beautiful in you, and I want to improve my life. I don't have to tear you down to get that quality, and the fact that you have it does not prevent me from having it as well" (Solomon & de Pont, 1985, p. 43).

Parents can use this approach so brothers and sisters can be helped to feel the "pie" is large, not small, reducing competition. It is far better to let a natural consequence take place than it is to punish our children.   Sometimes we are too impatient to wait for the consequences to appear, or because of some protocol, we are too weak to allow the universe to take its course. I remember how hard it was to let my eight-year-old go to school with poorly brushed hair. We were new in the town, lived in an odd loft building, and I was very concerned about what people would think of us. Yet I could not convince my girl that grooming carefully had value. She let her hair get hopelessly matted at the nape of her neck. Brushing hurt because it pulled. It was hard, but we let her classmates teach her about grooming.

The Parent As Giver of All Good and Perfect Gifts

Ideally a parent provides experiences for a child that teach and help the child develop mastery of various sorts. A good parent will teach that life is good and there is no reason to fear it won't remain good. A good parent will teach that problems can (must) be faced "head on" and can be mastered. We may not like the situations that have developed in our lives, but we can respond to them. It's unlikely we'll "die" from them.

The best gift a parent can give a child is his own mental health, to serve as a powerful model for the child in how to navigate life: "The single most important factor in effective parenting is making your life work. The single greatest gift you can give to a child is joyful participation in life. Perhaps the greatest curse on a child's life is growing up with the belief that life is cruel, defeating and hopeless. For this reason, it is vitally important to work on being an effective parent to yourself first. If you can give love, encouragement, support and fulfillment to the small child that most certainly lives within you, you are likely to parent your other children well" (Solomon & Ricioppo, 1985, p. 13). Do NOT SUCCUMB to the culture's idiocy: it's always been this way, so why bother?

Consistency

Small children need to count on regularity in their lives: "Consistency is often claimed to be the most important element in effective parenting. This means repeating an action in the same fashion every time. However, a person cannot sustain any effort that is not consistent with his character. It does not work for me to decide that I am never going to talk to my child when I am angry. That is a noble intention, yet unless I become a person who knows how to control my anger, I will not be able to refrain from losing my temper when my children misbehave. Techniques alone do not work. Changing my character does work" Solomon & Ricioppo, 1985, p. 10).

Paul Solomon explains the highest goals of parenting, empowering the child. It's a job in which, if we do it well, makes us become obsolete: "Each person alive today, from the time of childhood throughout adulthood, has two very important needs: to regularly receive concentrated attention from others, and to have some degree of control over the immediate environment. Supporting independence in a child means providing ways that he can feel in charge of his life and himself" Solomon & Ricioppo, 1985, p. 53).

<u>Discipline Issues</u>

While we do want to socialize children, we don't want to frighten them – they're already quite vulnerable: "When you disapprove of a child's action, make that very clear. Then immediately make clear to him that it is all right for him to make mistakes, and you still love and approve of him. Disapprove of the action, and know that it is all right for him to make mistakes. Discipline should never be administered in any other way. Whatever time or effort or inconvenience it might require to communicate clearly the difference in who he is and what he did will make an enormous difference in his self-image and his opinion of self-worth. Recognize the difference yourself, and the point out that difference to the child.

"It is equally important to point out the same thing about the child's positive behavior. Almost everyone in our culture is trying to gain self-worth by succeeding. If I make enough money, then I am a worthwhile person. If make an impression on society, if I do a great job, if I accomplish great things, then I have proved my worth, my validity as an individual. When a child accomplishes something wonderful, it is important to point out to him that is a wonderful thing to have done. 'That is great and I want you to know that your are great even without that accomplishment'.

"In working with the child's beliefs, and trying to change them, it is important to not be too grandiose. Speak in a way the child can accept…If the subconscious is already filled with a belief that 'I am ugly', it will probably respond to the affirmation, 'You are beautiful' with 'No, I'm not.', once again reaffirming its own belief. So it will take carefully constructed affirmations which can be accepted such as, 'I see the beauty in your ability to care for your friends, and it is growing stronger every day'. Choose something that is true, that the mind can hear. Do not fabricate" Solomon & Ricioppo, 1985, p. 53).

With Young Toddlers

Toddlers may have built a lot of emotional tension all day being "good, " especially in a day care or school placement. Even though the parent is tired at the end of the day, he must try to be kind and understanding with the child. Children don't understand adults' needs and time frames. They certainly have no idea what we need to accomplish in a day.

Imagination

Encourage imagination in your children. They will need to use wit and imagination in this changing world all of their lives. When reading a story with your child, play a bit and help the child imagine other developments or endings in the story. Talk with him or her while the family is watching television. Give your viewpoint on a situation and solicit that of your child. Much of the harm of television could be ameliorated if a parent would help a child give material a context, help him to understand what to think of what is seen.

Keep a box of "props" and costumes for children to play with. Even an old blanket can become a magic rug or tent. Play with them occasionally. A child badly needs the message that adult life is not all "gloom" and responsibility. So many adults present such a dark face to life that children express they do not want to grow up. Parents have no idea how often young people express to therapists that they do not want to grow up.

If a parent has no "playing" skills, the therapist may want to demonstrate them for the parent and play with the child, allowing the games to have a free flow and evincing enjoyment.

Teach a child to just "be." Many psychologists have taken exception to the patterns in our culture of trying to own many things, or have many accomplishments so we ARE something. John Bradshaw says we're all human-doings, not human beings. We cannot build real self-esteem in these ways, yet people try again and again. All one can be is what he already is. And that is good. Each one of us has a totally unique DNA grouping, a unique personality, unique abilities, and even unique lacks. We look different. No one else can be the other person any better than he is being himself. We are totally unique. So all of the hierarchies and possessions and competitive accomplishments are not really filling the limbic system needs. You can never get enough of what you really don't want. Taking the time to play in a non-directive way can encourage children to think for themselves and value time with close others.

In play and physical sensation, children learn to experience the world. In schools we try to change this to learning verbally, with very mixed results. Children, like all of us, are drawn to enjoyment, not conflict, so it is vital to make learning as enjoyable as possible.

Parents can help develop learning plans for their children. How a child mediates his world: experientially, visually, auditorially, musically, can be noted by the parent. In play, try to understand how the child is best responding. What is the child's style of play when he is able to choose, when he is at home? Is the child fond of tactile experiences? Is she interested in playing sports? Watching television? Listening to music? The child is drawn to what is the most compelling learning style for him. Those are our clues as to what will best work for the individual. We should learn ourselves, and use them. A good in-home therapist can help facilitate play between a child and his parent, and help teach the parent something about learning styles.

Spoiling the Child

Spoiling a child can mean the parent is unable to accept the child's anger at him. It shows a lack of confidence in the self on the parent's part. The child needs the parent to be strong. Sometimes the parent must frustrate the child.

Some child psychiatrists think it is a fair requirement that before we even consider having a child we must have clearly decided: "I am doing well in life. I can actually assist another human being in surviving and being happy." I believe it's helpful to a child, who is helpless in so many important ways, to want something, to negotiate for it, and to then receive it. It is a good lesson to see that you have some input into your environment and can affect it. Do we want to teach kids nothing they do matters? And then deal with the attendant tragedy of a discouraged, depressed person?

There are frequent adult complaints that children seek to manipulate, to control situations. All of us do that. It's nothing to take offense at. We parents can win at the Manipulate-and-Control-Others game. We have more resources. We have more friends, more powerful friends. Officials are more likely to listen to us.

A supervisor-mentor I had long ago told me one very exciting thing to do in a game of tug-of-war is to let go of your end of your end of the rope. It will certainly unbalance and surprise the other player.

If you forget manipulation altogether, and really satisfy, and really nurture and support the child (or marital partner for that matter), that is a way of letting go of your end of the rope. You may find that there's not that much to fight about after all.

Children are greatly enriching. They are open. They feel everything is possible. They remind us of ourselves long ago, when we all felt that way. Our children want to feel that we are glad they are here. They want to be told again and again that it matters to us that they are here. It is easy enough to tell them that. Tell them.

Sibling Rivalry

Sibling rivalry can be offset if parents use sensitivity. Find the skills and unique qualities and even foibles of each child and celebrate them. Use a sense of wonder with the children. Be amazed by their abilities and curiosities.

Family meeting in which children and adults can safely air "gripes" can help. Parents must be able to hear something the do not want to hear, some complaints about their parenting and favoritism. Even if the parent does not agree with the child's complaints, he should listen in a serious and respectful manner, as he would want to be listened to.

Parents should spend a bit of private time each day with each child. It need not be a large block of time if they don't have a large block. One very warm mother who had few material resources showed me very sensitive parenting. She was very robust and warm. She had a huge, lavishly appointed bed. She kept a small notebook, like a steno pad. Each of her four children, all up in through their teens, had a page in the book. She noted fears, important events, accomplishments, general observations about each child daily in this book. Each child received 15 minutes of private time, no matter what was going on in the household, each day. He or she could cuddle with the mother in her bed, or sit on the edge of the bed as he got older. This was the audience with their mother. No interruptions were allowed, and very rarely did days pass without the child receiving this block of time. The result was that, well into their teens, her kids talked to her, and talked to her in a bold and open way. They disclosed many things to her that ordinarily children would not. They lived in a tough public housing neighborhood, but these adolescents remained "good kids."

Lying

When a child lies to a parent it should be confronted. Some lies are not harmful; the parent can see the child struggling to "save" his ego in a situation. But anything that breaks trust must be confronted. A child needs to know we all define ourselves by our word. It's how we negotiate all interpersonal relationships. To break that trust sends the relationship careening in "limbo". How do you develop expectations and hopes with this other, now that trust is broken?

Speak kindly to the child and don't demand humiliation as the cost of the bad behavior. Examine the feelings of the child. Does he feel parental expectations are too difficult? Does he fear rejection? Is he very rivalrous with a sibling or any other family member? Why is he feeling so insecure that he lies? Would more approval ameliorate the situation?

The child already feels badly if he lied in the first place. There was some need to lie. Handling the betrayal of trust with a great deal of anger is very counterproductive. Explore with the child what he was thinking before he lied to you. He probably CAN remember. He won't remember with you if it doesn't feel safe. We develop our moral convictions in an atmosphere of love and support, not shame and blame.

Children and Anger

Children will repress angry feelings. They are frightened of them. They are not sure how far the anger will go. They are not sure if other people feel this anger: "If I let this genie out of this bottle, will he shoot my Dad, will he burn our family's house down?"

Children will often make an effort to repress emotion to control the anger. And that becomes a problem. The "block" becomes very generalized. The senses of creativity, curiosity and wonder are also blocked. Positive emotions are also lost in the generalized block the person created for self-protection.

The child feels extreme anger will lead to extreme retribution in the family. Sadly, this is often true. The repression of the anger, however, is a betrayal of our own selves, our truths, our "hurt self". In order to survive, the child has betrayed and abandoned himself. He may be so angry at himself that he experiences psychosomatic symptoms. There may be intestinal problems, migraine headaches, asthma, etc.

Repressed anger can make a child move from being a child repressing anger to a little automaton. "Yes, sir, no sir." An automaton can even become a dangerous bigot who will harm others. Early teaching can often say God will punish you if you don't honor your mother and father and love your family. Such a person may decide to project the anger out onto a targeted group of "troublemakers". Society offers us scapegoats: black people, Jewish people, poor people, rich people, etc. Of course, it is not at all uncommon for an individual to repress anger at his family and then suddenly, out of "nowhere" attack them. Repressed anger is a "powder keg" which can easily explode at any time.

Parents can model for a child. Help the child see his thought process is normal. Help him be willing to identify the process. Use yourself: "Johnny, it made me very angry when you spilled food all over the table and left it for me to clean. It made me think you must not have very much respect for me." Then give yourself and the child a few moments to discuss the conflict, resolving the conflict always as only behavior and not as important as our deep feelings of love for each other which are not going to disappear.

Model for the child that even very good people feel frustrated and angry at times. It's not "the end of the world."

If you see your child expressing a low tolerance for frustration (i.e. a short fuse), help him. The frustrations only become larger as we grow older. He must be able to work with these feelings. Help him achieve mastery in areas in which he does have ability. Praise him and let him know that he is important to you as an individual. You are proud of him whether he brings home A's or D's. He's your child and he has forever changed your life for the better. Family now means something different. Holidays are forever after valuable and different. You love him.

Parents can apologize. We can be human, misbehave, speak too roughly, perhaps even hit. We can always wait until we are no longer angry and go to the person (the other partner or the child) and say we went over the proper boundary. We are sorry. This does not need to create a loss of authority. We can look very large indeed if we have the courage to say we are sometimes wrong. This, of course, is also a reasonable behavior for an employer. We do not need to lose our authority, we can gain authority in our honesty.

Children, acknowledging our greater power, often will "go underground" with their behavior when they are too controlled. This occurs in the home with punishments imposed from without. From the child's earliest years we must learn to negotiate with the child. He is going to inexorably become bigger; we will have to learn anyway.

Of course, a parent must wisely pick those areas that are safe to negotiate. Choose small areas that can build strength and mastery in the child. We are always trying to teach, not just to control. The child needs his sense of autonomy. He will one day have to negotiate life without us by his side.

Choose the areas of negotiation with sense. Although we must learn to negotiate, we must also remember, some things are clearly right and some are clearly wrong. A toddler cannot choose to play with a butcher knife. As parents, it is our first order of business to make this understandable to a developing child. We should never let our fears of being disliked or thought to be out of the social opinion on a matter to move us from our moral compass. What's right and true is important. To value truth, self, and others are the most important guidelines we can give a child. A child feels more secure if we are clear in stating what must be. A child who feels out of control or unsure feels comfortable with a well-made fence around him. It creates a sense of personal safety: I know I'm not feeling stable, at least someone around me is feeling stable enough and interested enough in me to see that I only spin so far out of control. Of course, any child will kick like mad against the fence, especially if this emotional, social fence has just recently been erected.

Teens are sometimes grateful to be able to blame a strict parent. It gets them "off the hook" if they are unsure, but want to maintain an appearance of bravado. They are "cool" but have these ridiculously strict parents. What can they do?

Often a child will not give us the satisfaction of showing he heard us and agreed with us. We'll simply see a change of belief acted out in a different behavior. Allow even the tiny young individual to maintain his sense of pride, to "save face", whenever possible. (Allow young people to save face in all venues. I have often looked at young people in team meetings concerning their mental health, kids who "failed" in a behavior modification milieu, and felt: "He CAN'T do what we want. He's not well enough, not able." Children frequently flush with new shame as the bad behavior is publicly discussed for protracted periods in meetings.

Too Much Control, Shaming Control

Parents must wield their power graciously. Otherwise, we have not created a "good" person, but a false person: "A child which always complies with the often idiotic and irresponsible demands of its parents and resists own impulses, will cripple its personality and become a meek and dishonest character" (Perls, 1969, p. 155).

We want to take only the amount of control we truly need, and we must try to do it kindly: "In this quest, CONTROL is one of the first things children learn that they need to learn. That was just one of the first things we found out when we grew up: we needed to get control of ourselves. But the imposition of control is the source of anger. the imposition of control on anger is the source of ever greater anger. Displacement of anger in the form of judgements and internal moral resolves results in the child learning to hate everybody else and eventually himself as well. That growing child learns this as a way to survive" (Blanton, 1991, p. 48).

This is not what we want to be giving our children as a life philosophy. Because of the huge disparity of power in parent/child, mate/mate, at times, boss/employee, the person who feels aggrieved, angry, may also go "underground". The less powerful person may not want to show his anger. He could, instead, keep breaking his word to the more powerful person. He might gossip and malign the person behind his back. He will find a way to sabotage the more powerful person.

Human Motivations

Slightly older children are responding to the same motivations discussed by the social psychologists in the 1930's. Even children as young as 5 or 6 years of age will be motivated by:

The desire to gain attention.

The wish to gain power.

The desire for revenge.

Indications of despair, displaying inadequacy.

Parents must respond to children as these motivations surface. The key is to not become too angry and upset by them. We need to recognize we are dealing with a separate human being, who has his own goals. It's perfectly normal. It does not mean our authority is not being respected. We must set the same boundary, but always remember to listen to what the other is saying.

We need to create a secure world for our children. Of course, this sometimes means opposing them, but they expect us to: "Children do not desire unlimited 'freedom'. Most children feel safer and more secure in a structure that is somewhat authoritarian than in no structure at all. Children need limits and feel anxious in their absence. This is one of the reason they test limits-to be certain they are there. They need to know that SOMEONE IS FLYING THE PLANE" (Branden, 1994, p. 193).

Teaching Patience

Teach patience by doing something with the child that takes time and patience. Baking is a good example. Ingredients must be carefully assembled and mixed. There is then a waiting period in which you may not know how the food will turn out and can't yet eat it. Do the process with patience and enjoyment and you will teach your child how to wait without unduly stressing yourself. Being able to wait is a very helpful lesson for later life.

Discipline

In parenting groups, parents have stated the following reasons they don't like to discipline their children.

My children won't love me.

I'm too tired, or too busy.

I'm afraid my child will run away.

I'm afraid the child will "use the system" and accuse me, the

parent, of something.

I fear I won't be able to defend myself against his arguing.

Clearly, these are issues of the parent's self-confidence and courage. There are problems in the relationships as well, or these thoughts would never have been voiced. Any strong child will sense those things and continue to "push" the envelope. It's actually a kindness to let the child know there are boundaries around his behavior. He knows he's young and impulsive. He's aware he may well get himself into a bad situation. It's good to know someone wiser with more experience cares enough for him to keep him safe. We also need to carry a type of moral authority with our children. They need to respect us. We don't want to send a child the message the adult caring for him is so feeble he/she is afraid of him. This feeble adult is all that stands between the developing child and the harsh and unpredictable world. The child needs to feel the parent is not feeble.

A child behaving in ways we once did as children can be threatening. It can trigger pain and shame we have not resolved. A parent who feels this type of upsetting emotion developing with his child can stop and reflect. What did happen to him as a child? Were there ways in which he "sold out" to get along in a family? Ways in which he unsuccessfully resisted? We need to try to link our experiences with the exaggerated upset we feel in the present time.

A parent who finds a very disturbing sensation from childhood activated without knowing what was involved can talk to relatives: aunts, uncles, siblings, anyone who might be able to help fill in the history.

It helps us to make sense of our odd responses. It helps to keep them in check, and it also helps us to feel compassion for ourselves when we again regard what we went through.

Always in treatment, we are trying to fill in pieces of the "puzzle" and figure out what has happened to the person.

School

School is often a very shaming experience for kids. Because peers can so often be seeking some type of "advantage" in the vast pecking order, a student is loath to display any weakness, anything that can be used against him.

I suspect adults in schools are sometimes afraid of the very angry kids, and purposefully turn a "blind eye" so they do not have to be involved in a confrontation. Especially boys tell me in counseling that they cannot afford to not fight back. It would instantly give them a reputation as soft, and lead to further attacks. Our culture is in a sad condition and I do find this believable. Worse, I don't have a solution for the kids. Get into another environment?

I would like to see a return to the neighborhood schools we had in the past. A school of less imposing size is not so intimidating to a child. It was helpful when we had teachers who knew parents in the neighborhood. The general zeitgeist of our culture seems to continually move away from situations that support neighborliness and brotherhood and we are paying a cost.

There are also problems with accommodating individual learning styles. Dr. Howard Gardner, the well-known Harvard psychologist has tried to help adults understand for years that there are other ways of looking at intelligence than standard testing considers. A student might have good interpersonal skills, good spatial perceptions, musical ability, good coordination, artistic ability. It's very difficult to measure a child's determination, his personal goals and character. Of course, history is replete with great individuals who appeared awkward and unable as children and adolescents. Students with unique learning styles are very often discouraged and not properly considered by lesson planning.

To avoid shaming in the schools, and to increase actual learning for students, Dr. Gardner explained the need for experiential learning. Children respond very well to inventive teaching. Some of these children are not as able to perceive material visually or even auditorially and display good recall. The learning curve goes up considerably when experiential learning is used.

Ideally, all adults in a child's life help him to grow. They will support him and stimulate curiosity and encourage him. They will support him and stimulate curiosity and encourage him. I will always remember a wonderful teacher from the Bank Street College's school (known for progressive educational approaches) who used ordinary experiences to teach in a very exciting way. He once took two plain plastic cafeteria trays and "made it rain" between them using ice and a heater. One tray became the atmosphere, the other the earth, and it rained upon the earth. A fine science lesson for my second grader.

I like Polly Berends' fantasy school, where every child's curiosity is nurtured: "If I were king of the schools, next to the nurse's office where children are sent for health emergencies, I would set up an office for learning experiences. I would advise teachers to be on the lookout for passion fits or enthusiastic seizures. Whenever interest rose like a fever in a child-whatever the interest and whoever "afflicted" (retarded, gifted, or average) I would have her sent to this office. If during math she doodles dinosaurs, if going to the library she selects a book about dinosaurs, I would consider her a bit flushed and in need of immediate attention. Unlike the nurse, whose concern would be to see the temperature go down, the resource person in the Office of Learning Emergency would be concerned to gently huff on the glowing coal of her passion" (Berends, 1983, p. 121-122).

Working With Adolescents

Teach parents to listen and listen some more to their teenagers. Many times a kid is struggling with the same type of existential issues that bother adults: "This is not fair. This shouldn't be happening to me. Why did this happen to me? I want my life to be easy like it was last year. I don't want to face this, why must I? I have a right to be angry. I don't want to deal with my anger." Help young people see that we all suffer and look absurd at times. It happens to all of us, just at different times and in different ways. That is the human condition.

Teenagers, probably in part because of the sophisticated media to which they are constantly exposed, are no longer in awe of adults. This may "play out" as less respectful and seemingly entitled in a way prior generations never felt. This can be threatening to adults who must assert their authority. It has a positive aspect, however. The teenagers are less fearful and seem to have more confidence than we may have had at their ages. They may be stronger as they face issues in their lives. Another very important factor in teens' opinions of adults is that the kids have heard far too much adult business all of their lives. Children should be sheltered from many problems as they try to grow up. What is the value of exposing them to concerns about which they can do nothing?

A teenager will often work well with an older adult, and may seek advice from this adult on subjects they would not broach with a parent. Of course it is helpful if this adult has good values and lives a reasonable life himself.

The go-ahead, pull-back-and-hide struggle they are engaged in allows them to be very hypocritical and nasty with us. They are busy with the struggle and not thinking about our feelings and needs. They are feeling the "press" of impending adulthood very acutely.

The teenager will begin to attempt enhancing his self-esteem in the peer group. Parents are still important, but our opinions are not the most important thing any more. The youth knows he will have to "live" in this younger group in the future and we adults are becoming more irrelevant. This can be painful to a parent's self-esteem, but it need not be. It's easy to see that this moving out into the world is the natural order of things, a natural progression.

Teenagers still need boundaries and rules and they must be set by the parent. If they are disobeyed, state the rule again and insist that it is something you must have. As teens age, parents may want to re-visit some rules and see if there is some flexibility that could safely be shown. Try to not re-visit rules in the "heat of battle" as this teaches your child the rewards of "badgering" you.

Do not become gulled into a quarrel with a teenager who threatens to break a rule. Calmly state you do expect the rule to be obeyed. Do not take action until the rule is actually broken. Try to wield your power compassionately and recognize there are many, many minor behaviors that are not actually causing any great harm. Only address what you must address.

Your adolescent will mature. One day his own mature conscience will move him more than his desire for quick gratification. These are difficult lessons for all of us to learn. Half of our adult population has not yet learned it. Support your child as he comes to grips with the need to manage his mind and make his own moral and ethical and behavioral decisions. One day he will have to.

As they move toward adulthood in what cannot be argued is a frightening world, they feel an acute pull. On one hand, they want us to continue to take care of them. They like being carefree and irresponsible. They do not want to have to "try" for some goal and be seen as having failed. They are ashamed of this impulse to succeed, which is then checked by fear, and try to hide it from us much of the time. At the same time, teenagers are excited by the autonomy soon to be theirs. They feel strongly what things they would do differently, what they would like their homes to be like, how they would approach work, etc.

Adolescents are very fearful about entering the "rat-race" we call adult life. They have huge tasks to achieve: finding a suitable mate, finding a remunerative and satisfying job. As they get older we can talk a bit more intimately with them about our own past struggles, especially those that ended happily. We can share fears that almost stopped us, and how we ultimately handled them.

Adolescents have many fears about their looks. They fear they will not measure up. Listen sensitively to their concerns and try not to offer false assurances. Be genuine with the child.

A teenager may fear his parent may die. He may feel this is childish, or embarrassing, and may hesitate to tell you this. If you have genuine health issues, cover them openly with your child. Especially older teens should be allowed an honest appraisal of situation. IF you are seriously ill, develop a plan for protection of the child with the child. Children (teens) feel guilty their first concern remains the very human "what about me?" If the fears about your health are groundless, tell the child. Try to determine together if some misunderstandings have caused the child to fear this.

The trick of getting teenagers to talk to you begins long before the teens. The parent must listen patiently to all of the seemingly endless "chatter" a healthy child will share at 5, 6, 7 years of age. The reward for patience then is an openness later, in the teens, when the child may be doing more dangerous things and you need to have his trust.

Bullies

When someone is unkind, it is always a statement that he is also unkind to the self. He is very upset with himself, ashamed of the self, and is unable to tolerate the feeling. The feeling holds great force and he feels he must project it off onto another. It's difficult to do when we are under attack, but it is important to remember that attack is a projection of the person's own pain. We certainly don't have to, don't want to, accept his negative assessment of us. We must remember our own worth and not have our self image shaken by his pain. People will try again and again to "up end" us. They don't know how else to lessen their own pain. (Of course, this remedy doesn't really work for them.)

This type of understanding can help our children deal with bullies. A first line of defense would always be avoiding them as much as possible, but barring that, we can see their pain behind the assault. We can at least tell the truth within ourselves: it's not really about us.

Bullies appear to be attracted to two types of children. Children who are confident and seem to be rather "happy-go-lucky" seem to annoy them, as such kids appear to have everything they don't. Obviously, those children who seem weak and ineffective make good targets for them, as they are unlikely to give them much of a fight.

Other tips for dealing with bullies include:
Assert yourselves. Tell the other to stop making fun of you. Tell them it is unfair and very mean.
Use humor and try to deflect the issue: "Yeah, I'm having a bad hair day."
Try to avoid and get away.
Try to get help. Give help to others being bullied if you can.
Use good self-talk. Remind yourself in your own mind: "I'm not really stupid."

Deflect the criticism of yourself: "Yeah, I'm black. That's pretty clear isn't it?"

Try to use your empathy skills: "I hate hearing you talk to Tom that way. That would really hurt me."

Reality Therapy

William Glasser developed Reality Therapy, which allows natural consequences to teach a person. His work has often been misrepresented. He was not suggesting punishing others, but letting the normal events of life unfold in a cause and effect manner.

Glasser on ineffective treatment: "You need laughter, not self-indulgent paining; companionship, not sympathy; and personal accomplishment, not dependence on those who earn a living from your misery" (Glasser, 1984, p. 214).

Glasser on taking control of your life: "The most important control-theory question is 'Is the criticizing and misery I am now choosing helping me to get what I want?' The answer to this basic question, which must be asked by anyone who wants to regain control of her life, is always no . . . If my wife had asked Susan, who was unhappy when they met (or even if Susan had asked herself), 'What do you want?' the answer very likely would have been 'I don't know.' This is, of course, impossible. As much as any of us may try to deny it, we always know what is in our albums. If, however, we become discouraged because we can't get what we want, we lose less control by pretending we don't know. As her marriage began to fail, Susan knew very well that what she wanted was a better marriage" (Glasser, 1984, p. 171).

By albums, Glasser is referring to our series of "pictures", or ideas in our heads of what would make a good life for us. Each of us has formulated ideas of what we want, even if we don't even consciously acknowledge it to ourselves. "Your picture album-in which you find love, worth, success, fun, and freedom-is the world you would like to live in, where somehow or other all your desires, even conflicting ones, are satisfied. None of us has a picture in his album of himself doing badly" (Glasser, 1984, p. 30).

Glasser elucidates what we do need to be able to do in life, and what almost no one in mental health treatment can do, is to be able to negotiate our way to a better situation, to be able to calmly work with fellow human beings: "Talking-or more accurately, negotiating-is all we have to work out our differences. People too often choose to suffer, complain, criticize, fight, get sick, act crazy, or use drugs, all in an attempt to control someone else (or themselves), rather than work out their differences through negotiation. When people deride counseling as ineffective, what they are saying is that they do not want to negotiate-they want to control" (Glasser, 1984, p. 179).

Glasser on controlling another: "But, keep in mind, those who follow, who seem as if they are being controlled, do so only as long as following satisfies them. When it no longer does, they not only stop following, the begin to struggle to gain or regain control of the situation. More often than not, this struggle is expressed in a variety of miserable behaviors, such as choosing to depress, or getting involved in a self-destructive illness such as heart disease" (Glasser, 1984, p. 40).

Glasser on what we want to be teaching our children: "Try as hard as possible to teach, show, and help your children to gain effective control of their lives" (Glasser, 1984, p. 188).

Modeling/Looking for Work

I have frequently been amazed at how inadequate the job seeking skills of teenagers (and some adults) can be. An adult must serve as an example to teenagers seeking work. Many other social situations have become quite difficult, as our society moves further and further away from even the most basic manners. Even middle class homes are not doing a good job of teaching social skills to children and adolescents.

Human resources specialists have noted some very extreme behavior, none of which nets a job. One applicant took the interviewer's proffered business card, crumpled it, and tossed it into the trash in the interviewer's office. Applicants have rested their feet upon the interviewer's desk. People have lit cigarettes without asking permission during interviews, even tossing the match onto the rug. Many job applicants cannot make eye contact. This does not inspire the employer to trust him, obviously. The floor being stared at is not going to be the one to hire him. The trainers in EST used to say, and I don't think they were joking, that the most serious communication you can make, one to the other, is to try to convince the other to give you some of his hard earned money-from his pocket to yours. Our teenagers don't yet take this seriously.

These examples, which have been published in newspapers, are humorous, but the fact that they are occurring indicate that the applicant lacks very simple social skills. An adult can mentor and help "walk" the person through the process, listing expectations. I have been surprised by what seems very obvious needs to be covered. It's clear and families spend less and less time together, and extended family members are not always nearby, kids are lacking this type of training.

People would rather avoid and hide, and lose an opportunity, than look foolish, even if the opportunity was one they wanted very badly. A good therapist can use the relationship to move the client toward smoother social behavior without shaming him. Humor is a great asset in these situations.

One of the great values of the In-Home services is that behavior can be tried out, in vivo. I am always pleased by how much difference even simple job coaching can make for kids. Many youths we see are badly under socialized; basic ideas simply do not occur to them. They are open to suggestions and would like to be spared social embarrassment (like all of us).

In Mobile Therapy work I had to teach a sixteen-year-old in a middle class household (the father was a successful politician) to use eating utensils. He ate most of his meals as cereal with a spoon. I took him to a diner, forced him to order something that had to be eaten with a knife and a fork, made sure our table was out in the middle of the restaurant, and well seen by others. I gently modeled the use of the utensils and talked him (softly, inaudibly to other diners) through the process. His parents had become so exhausted with his overly energetic and trying behavior they had long since given up this type of modeling. This slow, patient work, one on one, is what will succeed, however. I also taught this boy to pump gas. As adults we forget someone once taught us these things.

We coached an older, housebound girl (17) into attempting temporary work. She had been living in a darkened bedroom in a haze of copies of Cosmopolitan magazine. We helped her step by step through the application process and explained everything to her carefully again and again. She was applying for the most basic, beginning factory work, some type of sorting. On the appointed day our team drove her to the place of business listed on her job placement form. We arrived early and parked not too near the building so we did not embarrass her. We left. We called the next day to find out how she did. To our surprise she was at home again in the morning. We asked what had happened to her job. She explained that when she went up to the work building and checked the street number, there were two doors she could have taken. She didn't know which one to pick. So she chose neither. She called her mom and had herself picked up. Job over.

In working with teenagers in public, the therapist must be prepared for some personal embarrassment and be strong enough to deal with it. I was once with a teenaged girl who became enraged with a nurse in an Emergency Room who was teasing her in a passive aggressive manner. To my surprise, my client punched her on the jaw with a hard right hand, knocking the nurse off her feet, into the concrete wall. The mood in the room was suddenly very chilly and it was clear many people blamed me for the punch just as though I had thrown it. It was several months before I felt welcome in that hospital.

References

Berends, Polly. (1983). Whole Child, Whole Parent, NY, NY. Harper & Row

Blanton, B. (1991). Telling the Truth. Stanley, VA: Sparrow Hawk Publications.

Branden, N. (1994). Six Pillars of Self-Esteem. New York: Bantam Books.

Glasser, W. (1984). Control Theory. New York: Harper & Row.

Perls, F. (1969). Ego, Hunger and Aggression. New York: Random House.

Solomon, P. & de Pont, N. (1985). The Tao of Communication. Timberville, VA: The Master's Press.

Solomon, P. & Ricioppo, G. (1985). Feed My Little Lambs. Timberville, VA: The Master's Press.

CHAPTER FOURTEEN: SERIOUS ISSUES

Extreme Anger

American culture seems to grow more angry by the day. From road rage to domestic violence to school violence to government workers' and corporate leaders' misbehavior we see that people feel very sorry for themselves and then develop an odd sense of entitlement: because I have suffered so much, it's "o.k." for me to do this bad thing to another. Treatment of anger issues may be the single largest "symptom" that brings clients into treatment by their families.

Anger has value. It does exist for a purpose. It can get our energy going when we need it. Our brains evolved that way; there are times we need to galvanize our energy for our safety. Anger may be letting us know something is amiss and someone may be attempting to violate our rights or be doing something unjust. The body may respond with a sense of tension violation before our cognitive processes have been able to identify this. There may be some socially driven reason why the person's cognitive process may not be willing to identify a violation, but his BODY will respond. Our rising anger can convey a warning to the violator, a warning that may end the violation. In the animal kingdom, a creature might bare its fangs to warn another. The anger makes us feel more powerful. Obviously, the negative aspects of anger are well known.

Anger blurs our perceptions. It is more difficult to realistically assess a situation when our senses are bombarded with feelings of anger. We miss cues in the environment that might actually be helpful to us in solving the situation. We often will tend to see only the negative, only what is frightening, when we are angry. It is as though our vision is wearing a "filter."

Often anger allows impulses to take over the person. We may act before we know what has really happened. What has happened in those instances is that for some weeks or months the person has been ruminating in a negative way. He has a "chip on his shoulder" and has internally been shining and honing the anger, his right to the anger. The internal level of fear has thus risen. Then, when faced with any environmental cue that even remotely reminds him of the anger-provoking "grudge, " he will suddenly "blow." The impulse has actually been brewing for some time. The honing of the anger over time makes it more difficult for the person to resist his impulse. The universe must be "righted." He is angry.

Rather than feel hurt of ashamed over a situation, our egos encourage us to blame another and quickly project the anger out onto another person. This can, or course, create anger in the other person. It also keeps us from working with the original situation or belief that caused us to feel ashamed, increasing the chance we will again be caught in the same type of situation. There will be no mastery of the situation as long as we are avoiding it and using projection. In therapy, we must TELL THE TRUTH. It is the very first and necessary step to healing.

Anger creates for us a kind of false persona that we feel serves our needs. This can easily be seen in the popular "rap" music. If I am very afraid, I may feel it will be useful to appear to others to be very tough, very "bad." It is similar to the baring of teeth done by other mammals. The plan is to divert trouble by the tough appearance. In rap videos and our movies, very fearful characters are clearly assuming what they think are defensive postures, designed to avert trouble in the future. This false persona stresses revenge. How many of our movies have had a theme of revenge? How many of them seem to be pushing the belief that revenge is the best satisfaction one can attain in life? Our males would be in far better condition in this culture if clinicians would publicly identify these personas as needed only by weak and fearful individuals, nothing to be admired.

In the body, chronic anger may lead to heart trouble, hypertension, even some cancers. Lowered immune system function is thought to be related to anger. Bowel and stomach tension and their attendant disorders feed upon anger. Behavior always makes sense if we look at the angry person's core beliefs. People are running a type of dialogue:

It's really awful that you treated me this way.

I can't stand being treated so badly and disrespectfully by you.

You dare not treat me this way.

You are an awful person to treat me this way.

Since you are an awful person, unlike innocent me, it's "ok" for me to do this to you.

Many therapists regard that fear is at the core of all anger. The anger is a "busy-making" action to avoid dealing with the fear. Often the anger is an action that will help protect us from that which is feared. Some Common Core Fears are:

I am afraid of dying.

I am afraid of growing old.

I am afraid of being mediocre or not mattering.

I don't want to be ineffective.

I am afraid of being ill.

I am afraid of not having love or of losing the love I have.

I want to be close to others, but I am afraid to.

I am afraid of being poor.

I am afraid of not being free. I have had so many disappointments, I may need to "run."

I am afraid of not being in control.

I am afraid of exposure.

I am afraid people will see my needs and hurt me.

I am afraid of being criticized.

We will take angry action to hide from these very normal and common fears. People develop a shame and fear that only I feel these fears. Others will laugh at me, or feel superior to me if they suspect what I am really feeling.

Criticism is more painful for people than most of us realize. The one mistake I have made again and again, both clinically and in my personal life, is to overestimate the amount of strength people have. They are not as strong as I like to believe. Paul Solomon taught me that if you are going to criticize someone, make the criticism like a nice big sandwich. He is less hesitant to eat. Put two big, fluffy pieces of bread on either end. In the middle, put a tiny, thin slice of meat.   The meat is the information that may be difficult to accept. The bread is praise for him: what is good, what is working well. This is a wonderful "formula" for any situation. A criticism is the most difficult kind of communication we have to deliver.

Anger is fueled by our irrational beliefs. We "pound" ourselves again and again in our own minds. We cause ourselves to feel that only we have limitations and faults. Some common limiting beliefs are:
I must do everything perfectly.
I am not allowed to be afraid.
I can never cry.
I must be approved of at all times by everyone.
The world is unsafe.
I can never get angry.
I can never tell what goes on (went on) in our family. It's too horrible.
I am not allowed to be afraid.
There is something very wrong with me. Only I have this fault.
I must hide this "wrong" or others will fall upon me and destroy me.

Our cognitive minds, especially with assistance from someone kind, of course, realize that we cannot meet these weird "demands, " but we allow them to drive fears in us nonetheless.

Very angry children require extra care by parents. Any trouble with the law is a very serious matter. In terms of attitude a parent or clinician should regard a crime against a person or animal as more problematic than a crime against property, although both are serious. Any anti-social behavior should be immediately dealt with.   If something is taken from a store, give a child a chance to "clean the slate." Go with him and take the item back to the store. If it feasible, have the child do some work for the storeowner. Help the child to understand the storeowner has responsibilities and needs himself. He is taking care of a family. People depend upon him for their livings. He has to pay for the merchandize himself. It's not free. Taking his merchandize hurt everyone in the "chain." Let the child know he may even know some of the affected children of these families himself. We are a community.

Do not go overboard on punishment. A month of "grounding" is impractical (the parent can't stand it) and will create anger toward you. This much time grounded will also cause the child to forget the original infraction; he will be focused on how harsh his parents are.

Work with your child to build his new self-esteem. You don't want him getting attention and recognition from a youth gang. Unfortunately, these gangs will meet his needs if you don't meet them in the family. There are few rituals and initiations to help a young person enter adulthood. Create them in the family with love. Don't let some street "thugs" create an initiation for your child.

Dr. Randell Curren of the University of Rochester is quoted in The New York Times as stating: "The best predictors of which children will graduate into a more permanent pattern of crime are their likelihood of being unemployed after leaving school and the amount of violence in their families" (Kutner, 1993, Section C, p. 10).

Help your child feel the world will meet his needs and is interested in him. People who have something to lose will not take sad risks. Social psychologists said behavior is motivated by: power, control, revenge, and to cover deficiency. It may be that what we call misbehavior begins when a person consistently feels powerless, a total lack in his ability to play any part in his own destiny. Anger becomes hard to control when we perceive huge gaps between what we want and what we have, and especially, what we'll always have.

American culture feeds desire. Whatever one has achieved, there is one up on the rung of the ladder above him. We are always looking one notch up, regarding the place we are occupying as bad, not enough, not good enough. The culture teaches us that the individual is responsible for his own failure. Really "good" people are always rich and successful. This further creates anger, as the person finds this so painful he is likely to project blame out onto another. This projection is key to understanding our "angry white males." They fear it is "them" and project this anxiety out as anger as quickly as possible.

Psychiatrist Wilhelm Reich talked of the "emotional plague character" as an ordinary man who is actively destructive toward the expressions of life in self and others. Early limbic pain, and the armoring the individual did against the pain, creates a distorted, vicious person who will explode into destruction to release his tension and feel SOMETHING. Feeling anything is regarded by the "emotional plague character" as far preferable to the greyed-out depression in which he exists.

The great sociologist Paul Goodman talked of the cruelty of the society as a group and its harsh treatment of increasing numbers of unassimilable minorities. The great psychologist Erich Fromm spoke of the herd mentality, and how a man will deny what his own eyes tell him in order to remain in the group. Only a person who can tolerate social ostracism is likely to feel a solidarity with humanity. It does require emotional and spiritual development.

The excellent work of Gordon Allport moved us to a good understanding of hatred and prejudice: "As one example, we may cite the convictions of the philosopher Hobbes, who sought the roots of prejudice in the unsavory instinct of man. So that in the nature of man, we find three principles causes of quarrel. First, Competition; Secondly, Diffidence; thirdly, Glory. The first maketh men invade for Gain; the second, for Safety; and the third, for Reputation. The first use violence to make themselves masters of other men's persons, wives, children and chattel; the second to defend them; the third for trifles, as a word, a smile, a different opinion, and any other sign of undervalue, either direct it in their persons, or by reflection in their kindred, their friends, their nation, their profession, or their name.

"Hobbes is here saying that the sources of conflict lie in (1) economic advantage, (2) fear and defensiveness, (3) desire for status (pride)" (Allport, 1954, p. 214).

Allport's sense of humor explains human behavior in the following anecdote: An enterprising pig with some ducks as companions is aloft in a rudderless balloon. A farmer with evil intentions is trying to capture the balloon, but the alert piglet pelts the farmer with cans of tomato soup. The farmer is splattered by the soup and thoroughly angry. A dirty-faced boy comes out of the barn to help him wipe off the soup. But the farmer cuffs the little boy good. He does this for three reasons: First, because the balloon had got away; and second, because he would now have to take a bath to get the sticky soup off him; and third, because it seemed like a pretty good thing to do anyway" (Allport, 1954, p. 349-350).

It's painful to look at our own shortcomings; the other is always more interesting: "We have already indicated that extropunitiveness may be a trait of personality. Some people look constantly for alibis. Hitler was such a person. He blamed the bad world, a bad school, fate, for his many failures in early life. When he did not pass in school, he blamed illness. For his political reverses, he blamed others. For the defeat at Stalingrad, his generals. For starting the war, he blamed Churchill, Roosevelt, the Jews. There seems to be no record of his blaming himself for any missteps or failures.

"There is something exhilarating about extropunitive indignation. To be good and angry at someone else, or even at fate, is like being on a spree. The joy is twofold. Partly it is a physical relief from pent-up tension and frustration. Partly it is restorative of one's own self esteem. Not I but others are wholly at fault. I am blameless, virtuous, more sinned against than sinning" (Allport, 1954, p. 383).

Cults, Hatreds

Arthur Deikman identified unhealthy social behaviors (Reich's Character Defect Man) as being rampant in America. Many of us, even in respected groups, evince the personal weakness that lead to a cult-like devotion to a group ethic. We are quite ready and able to abandon our personal moral compass, if we have one: "If you still feel immune from cult influence, I can offer a checklist of everyday behaviors that you may recognize all too well:

1. Speaking of adversaries or outsiders (e.g. conservatives, liberals, Yuppies, blue collar, rich, poor) as if the were all the same; characterizing them by negative traits only; attributing unflattering motive to them but not to oneself.
2. Lacking interest and information concerning the actual statements and actions of opponents or outsiders.
3. Failing to consider the possible validity of an adversary's point of view.
4. Not taking a critical look at one's own position.
5. Disapproving or rejecting a member of one's group for departing from the group position, devaluing the dissident, regarding him or her as an annoyance or a problem.
6. Feeling self-righteous" (Deikman, 1994, p. 154).

Obviously, here Deikman is talking about, and it remains a recurring theme in all treatment, empathy for others or lack of empathy for others.

Of course it's people's relationships to themselves that cause them to feel angry at others in their world: "Commenting on the admonition to love they neighbor as thyself, longshoreman-philosopher Eric Hoffer remarks somewhere that the problem is that this is precisely what people do: persons who hate themselves hate others. The killers of the world, literally and figuratively, are not known to be in intimate or loving relationship to their inner selves" (Branden, 1994, p. 48).

Teenagers are obviously working toward independence. They are torn between the desire to be taken care of, and the real need to move toward a life outside of the family. Males will often "hide." They are struggling with fears and conflicts and don't want them seen by others, especially the parents who might question them about it, further exposing "weakness." Acting out hides fears. It delays the need to examine and work with the fears for the acting-out person. If the fears feel too large, too beyond solution, one way of coping is to create behavior that requires attention, deflecting pressure from the lurking fears. Most teenagers are deeply shamed by their fears. Our culture stresses the rugged individual (who, of course, doesn't exist) the teflon man who sheds all anxieties and pressures without blinking. Our kids feel only they are frightened and controlled by their fears.

Clinicians have had good results by giving young people a checklist, helping them to identify what is at issue:

Worry about achievement, grades, college or job.

Adults who embarrass them: parents or teachers, employers

Parents who are critical of their friends and might embarrass them.

The loss of a friend (sometimes, now, even to death).

Teasing by peers; people saying painful things.

Being overwhelmed by the demands of life: work, schoolwork, work at home.

Worry about the well-being of a parent.

Pressures and temptations of sex, drugs, alcohol

Feeling depressed.

Not feeling able to talk with anyone. No one understands. It's so bad I dare not tell anyone.

Siblings who hurt their feelings, are favored, make them angry, even harm them.

Parents quarreling and even being physically violent.

Parents ignoring, especially in separated families.

As the clinician or parent moves further and further away from his adolescence, a list like this is sometimes helpful. Ideas can be "bounced off" the client to stimulate discussion and help determine what are the difficult areas for the client. Some of these issues might not seem that serious to the clinician, but kids can often become quite distraught and histrionic, even suicidal over them. The kid's world is different. We become upset over job and relationship loss. School and peers are the world to adolescents.

Girls will pick battles with parents in an effort to move away without the severe risk of actually physically moving away. Most middle class kids are well aware that they could not live well on their own. They are well aware they might consign themselves to an underclass life of misery if they forego the help parents can continue to offer.

A great deal of fault finding of parents occurs. At her zenith, my teenaged daughter commented on my appearance every single day. "you're NOT wearing THAT, are you?" Well, I have it on . . . the kids are trying to "cut the parent down to size." They want to emotionally move away from them. They need to find their own mates and create their own home. They are developing and sharpening their own beliefs. They are busy trying on and off identities and "ways of being, " almost like costumes. We should not concern ourselves too much with piercings and hair colors unless a child is impeding health in some way. It is more likely to pass into fad oblivion if we do not respond too greatly to a fad tried.

The tasks that must be mastered by an adolescent are daunting, daunting to all of us. They must find a good and loyal mate. They must find satisfying and remunerative work. They must find a way, in other words, to join the adult "rat race" that grows ever more competitive, and not be trampled in the process.

A parent should not fight every last battle with a teenager. Go for the "maximum get-able" without too much quarreling. Ignore threats of disobedience. Deal only with actual disobedience. The adult will completely wear himself out otherwise. Following an infraction of the rules, always remind the child of the same rule. It is still in effect and you do expect him to respect it.

Doing Treatment with Very Angry, Anti-Social Teenagers

The anti-social acts done by kids are often thought of as an effort to break back into a world that seems to have locked them out. In working with such an adolescent, test for some area of vulnerability. Is there anyone whose feeling he does care for? His mother? His girlfriend?

Speaking softly is a good idea. Speaking slowly reflects a calmness the session will be helped by. The therapist must clearly display he/she is not afraid of the client. Make eye contact with this person. If a situation becomes very "dicey, " it's probably better to just end the session that day. This gives the client back some power and helps clear strong feelings simply by having a time interval.

Some therapists feel it's not helpful for an angry person to punch a bag to express anger. It may simply fuel anger. I am not sure the release is not helpful. The ideal thing for this client is an affective reprocessing of the anger if he will allow it. Very "small doses" of affective work will be accepted by all but a few clients.

Angry Teens and School

Educator Leon Botstein has recently offered some remedies for the struggle teenagers have with school. He proposes cutting high school shorter and allowing a youth to enter college, a vocational program, or even an arts program, at age sixteen. We are increasingly having difficulty convincing students that school has any relevance for later life. Truancy continues to be endemic.

I agree with those who feel there is a body of knowledge that people should have to be reasonably educated. Perhaps we would be more successful in imparting that "body" to a dancer in art school, or a boy showing mastery at welding. So much of the school experience is shaming for those not doing well, and boring for those who are being taught "down to" to help others in the class.

Let kids follow their special interest and loves, and then try to "sneak in" some of the body of knowledge. They will be more accepting if the whole school experience is not as shaming. Some "mastery" experience of competence, in welding, would help a boy deal with English literature.

Adoption

During adolescence the teenager who has been adopted faces especially difficult issues. He needs, developmentally, to break away from his family. Yet he has already been given away once before.

Sometimes an adopted child will hurt his/her parents' feelings by lashing out and saying: "I don't have to listen to you. You're not even my real parents." This can certainly be very painful for adoptive parents to hear. Try to remember that adolescents will use these lines on their biological parents as well. Try, and it can be difficult, not to take these histrionic attacks too personally. Some teens will even go so far as to seem to be pushing the adoptive parents to say they will "give them back." They really want to know the home is a safe and very secure place for them. They need to be told again and again: you will never be rejected or abandoned.

All of us, at times, in relationships, play what I call the "Do You Love Me?" game. They keep annoying and testing, testing. Marital partners will absolutely do this. Do you love me if I? How about if I? The person will keep upping the ante. Of course, the only answer they ever want to hear is "Yes, yes, yes." Unfortunately, people CAN exhaust one another. It is do-able. Hopefully the exhaustion will only be temporary.

Always, for the adopted child, the underlying dynamic is: Someone didn't want me. I wonder why. I wonder who they were? I wonder, if they really knew me, would they change their minds? The children must be encouraged to focus their attention on the fact that someone DID want them, and very badly. Chose them, even.

Cutting

There are a number of people who are presently engaging in moderately serious self-mutilation behaviors. They may be burning themselves, cutting themselves, pulling hairs from the body, sticking the body with needles or other sharp objects, even chewing glass or rubbing glass into the body. One of the worst situations I saw involved a boy who broke up light bulbs and then ate the glass.

Incidents may continue for years and do usually increase somewhat in severity. Often other addictive behaviors, anorexia or bulimia, or various substance abuse tendencies are also in place.

Some doctors feel the current social acceptability of body piercing makes this behavior more likely to occur.

Clients insist that the mutilation makes them feel better. The physical pain helps obfuscate a more intolerable psychological pain. It can break through numbness, making the person feel more alive. It is a way of breaking through depression.

Mutilation is practiced most frequently by white women, but we are beginning to see more of it in other populations.

Many clients report the cutting acts as pressure valve for them. If gives them an action to take when the stresses of life are extreme. There is an implicit cry for help in the mutilation. "Maybe someone will notice I am upset and tend to me."

The mutilation gives the person a sense of control. The body symbolically carries many guilt feelings. It is clearly the "sinner." If there was abuse of a physical or sexual nature, it was played out upon the "guilty" body. A client may be attempting a kind of purification ritual, using the same battleground, the body. This is a type of magical thinking, and only postpones the pressure the client is feeling. Cutting can release endorphins. The body responds to the pain and releases them to help. This cycle can become addictive.

Cutting gains some notice. I do exist. If I can be damaged, I do exist. We should always take these expressions of pain seriously. Treat the client for affective issues, sadness and anger. Since teens have a taste for the macabre and gruesome I will tell them: "If you kill yourself while on my caseload, I'll dig you up and kill you twice." (Obviously, I use such joking judiciously.)

Standard crisis treatment discusses suicide and the questions that should be asked. What has caused life to not be worth living? The more reasons the person can provide, obviously, the higher the risk to the patient.

How much do you want to live?

How much do you want to die?

How often do you have these thoughts?

Have you ever attempted suicide? All attempts or gestures should be noted.

How long ago did this or these attempts occur?

Has a family member or friend ever committed suicide?

What plan do you have to accomplish this? Is anyone assisting you? Where will you do this? Ask the probability of this occurring on a scale from one to ten.

Ask the person if there is anyone he trusts enough to prevent this. Try to get a name and a reach number for this person.

Eating Disorders

One of the best books on eating disorders is the classic work <u>Fat is a Feminist Issue</u> by Susie Orbach. Her books contain wonderful affective exercises as well. What does the client feel like in a large room with a slim body? How do people react to her? How safe does she feel? What does the fat body do for her? How do people react to her? How does she dress, etc.

The way a girl sees her mother and her mother's power or lack of power affects her attitudes about her body and about becoming a woman. Additionally, it has long been thought that eating disorders are related to past sexual abuse. A fat body presents a solid wall of protection for the sexual organs. A thin body may be so thin an abuser doesn't notice it and will leave her alone: "And so, too, women with eating disorders dwell on their past, recalling their childhood in a way that suggests they blame themselves for the suffering of their mother . . . for this reason, a feminist analysis is frequently so liberating for these daughters, who otherwise fail to see themselves as part of a generation struggling for development their own mothers lacked" (Chernin, 1985, p. 64).

Clinicians see a deep ambivalence about the female role: "They all are deeply preoccupied with making some return to their mother for the sorrows and deprivations they believe they have caused" (Chernin, 1985, p. 66).

When girls view their mothers, they experience disappointment and fear about being a female in the world: "At a moment when serious political gains have won and women are able to take up the opportunity for further development, there is a marked tendency among women to retreat, to experience a failure of nerve, a debilitating inner conflict about accepting advantages and opportunities denied to their mothers" (Chernin, 1985, p. 43).

As noted in many theories on anorexia, a reluctance is noted to move into adult life and be a woman: "An eating disorder is, in fact, an extremely effective way to stop the movement into the world" (Chernin, 1985, p. 21).

We do see this, as gains for women are made in the world, it takes a measure of courage to claim the new gains. Many girls are lacking the ego strength, and preoccupy themselves with the struggle over appearance. Chernin discusses how girls have become disillusioned and anxious about the female role: "And soon there comes before the child, in place of the omnipotent magical mother of infancy, the mother in reality-a woman who is, let us say in conflict about maternity, longing for a self-development that she has not achieved and that the birth of a child will make even more elusive, a woman frequently harassed, sometimes depressed, often distraught" (Chernin, 1985, p. 121).

People ascribe magical qualities to the substance of food. No substance can possibly deliver such a rescue: "Much of the obsessive quality of an eating disorder arises precisely from the fact that food is being asked to serve a transformative function it cannot carry by itself, although in earlier, tribal cultures food was always an essential part of those transformative collective ceremonies through which individuals were brought, step by step, to separate from one phase of their development and enter the collective" (Chernin, 1985, p. 167).

Women are showing a clear ambivalence about the future: "Women today seem to be practicing genocide against themselves waging a violent war against their female body precisely because there are no indications that the female body has been invited to enter culture" (Chernin, 1985, p. 186).

Thus, the food re-enacts a kind of self-dislike at being a body that is not invited to enter culture. The food is asked to fulfill a magical role indeed: it is to be a balm for any and all emotional hurts. Carol Bloom, an excellent therapist from New York, used to say eating when you are sad, or angry, is simply inappropriate: like putting french fries on a cut.

On Behavior Modification

Alfie Kohn has written a very interesting book on the failure of behavior modification as it is currently practiced. Our failed prison-industrial complex is the most glaring example of this failure, but many school districts and home programs show the same results. Mr. Kohn is not surprised we like these programs in America. We are a practical, "get on with it" people. We are pioneers and entrepreneurs with no time for excuses and theories. We like plans that promise "Do A and you'll get B." End of story. On a more troubling note, too many of these programs put one person in the role of overseer and the other as owned property. The overseer does not have to bring too much thought to the process. All he has to do is make demands.

Take only minimal control. The parent will tire, and the child will wait for this moment and move into the vacuum. Take only what control you must have in any given circumstance. This is true for parents, employers, teachers, anyone who must wield power.

Kohn talks about the punishment that rewards in a behavior modification system can become. "The first derives from the fact that rewards are every bit as controlling as punishments, even if they control by seduction" (Kohn, 1993, p. 51).

People feel coerced and controlled when they are being coerced and controlled: "Except for the places where their use has become habitual, punishments, and rewards are typically dragged out when somebody thinks something is going wrong. A child is not behaving the way we want; a student is not motivated to learn; workers aren't doing good work-this is when we bring in the reinforcements.

"What makes behavioral interventions so terribly appealing is how little they demand of the intervener. They can be applied more or less skillfully, of course, but even the most meticulous behavior modifier gets off pretty easy for one simple reason: REWARDS DO NOT REQUIRE ANY ATTENTION TO THE REASON THAT THE TROUBLE DEVELOPED IN THE FIRST PLACE" (Kohn, 1993, p. 59).

What are we really trying to teach: integrity, confidence, moral judgment and common sense: "THE LONG TERM GOALS WE HAVE FOR OUR CHILDREN. What would we like them to be able to do, to want to do, to feel, to be like in the years to come? Invariably, what I hear is a desire for children to be self-reliant and responsible but also socially skilled and caring, capable of surviving and succeeding in life yet willing to question and think in a creative and critical manner, confident and possessed of an unshakeable faith in their own worth while still being open to criticism and new ideas.

"The unsettling news is that rewards and punishments are worthless at best, and destructive at worst, for helping children develop such values and skills. What rewards and punishment do produce is TEMPORARY COMPLIANCE. They buy us obedience. If that's what we mean when we say they 'work', then yes, they work wonders" (Kohn, 1993, p. 161).

Anything that we teach in anger creates more difficulties than it solves: "Regardless of what we are trying to get across by spanking, paddling, or slapping them, the messages that actually come through are these: 'Violence is an acceptable way of expressing anger' and 'If you are powerful enough you can get away with hurting someone.' For decades, researchers have consistently found that children subjected to physical punishment tend to become more aggressive than their peers, and will likely grow up to use violence on their own children. These effects are not confined to victims of what is legally classified as abuse: even 'acceptable' levels of physical punishment may perpetuate aggression and unhappiness" (Kohn, 1993, p. 167).

Of course, this is because of the damage inflicted to the child's limbic system, damage that rests in the mind and the body, and will last a lifetime.

Mr. Kohn makes his point well that we need to deal with motivation: "Once again we have to ask what our ultimate goals are. Do we want only to control short-term behaviors, or do we want to help children become responsible decision -makers? To choose the latter is to say that motives matters: we care about not only what children do, but why they do it. The more we attend to these issues, the less likely we will be to defend an approach that says, 'If you do something bad, here's what I'll do to you.'" (Kohn, 1993, p. 172).

Our burgeoning prison-industrial complex is hardly an American success story: "Indeed, if an auditorium were filled with bank robbers, wife batterers, and assorted other felons, we would likely find that virtually all of them were punished as children. Whether the punishments were called 'consequences' is irrelevant: what matters is that these people were trained to focus not on what they were doing and whether it was right, but on what would happen to them if someone more powerful didn't like what they did" (Kohn, 1993, p. 172).

Kohn suggests that misbehavior gives a "teachable moment" and two people can review the situation together and problem solve. Something has gone wrong, and two people need to think about it. By this approach, it can be conveyed to the misbehaving person that more is expected of him and the other person has confidence he will develop better coping skills. The person will try to live up to the trust. Kohn says scolding and scolding is like saying: "I've typed and typed and I STILL haven't produced a good book, clearly, typing doesn't work" (Kohn, 1993, p. 233).

He admits that it takes patience and self-restraint to work through problems with people, and suggests that if people continue to not comply with a request, the nature of the request should be examined. The individuals involved need to explore: is any compromise possible? Some negotiators call it looking for a win-win: "This perspective can be highly threatening to people whose premise is that others should simply do what they are told. Their preferred question is, 'How can I make them?'- a question whose answer is invariably couched in behavioristic terms. Parents may feel this way even more acutely than managers or teachers do because in no other arena do we take for granted so asymmetrical a relationship as that between parent and child" (Kohn, 1993, p. 234).

In examining our requests, Cohn wants us to consider if we are asking something that conflicts with a child's basic drives. Are we asking for silence and stillness from young children? Are we demanding that they not express emotion? Are we requiring a teenager to not be interested in his peers? He cautions us to not demand mindless obedience to "mindless restrictions." At the very least we owe a child a good, full explanation of why we want what we want. He says we will fare better with any decision if we "Bring the kid in on it." We want to work with others in a collaborative process to mitigate conflict.

In the very moving biography of his brother, executed killer Gary Gilmore, his brother, Mikel, reviewed Gary's failed life. In <u>Shot in the Heart</u>, Mikel searches for the one moment when everything went wrong. He finds the truth to be even worse: that all the moments made a difference and too many of them were bad. Another brother from the family explained that the brutal punishment from the father would never make a man sorry for what he had done. He compared the beatings they took to castrating a man because he had shoplifted a loaf of bread. The punishments would not make him feel sorry he took someone's bread, depriving him. Rather, he will feel hatred because he was mutilated for a lousy loaf of bread.

Children in Placement

Quincy Howe Jr. wrote an excellent book on placement called <u>Under Running Laughter</u>. He recognizes the crushing depression under acting-out behavior. He talks about what an affront it is to a child to know that the one who gave birth to him is out somewhere doing ordinary activities while he, the child, languishes in placement, raised by hired others. Howe says if the children are going to be made whole again at all, it will be by the patient nurturing day in and day out by those who have the child in care.

How handy it is that we can now blame biology for our children's sadness and anger: "It makes eminent sense that parents of a biologically handicapped child should not (as has been true in the past) be regarded with suspicions as themselves causative, it is also true that parents who have in fact been cruel would be equally attracted by the posture of 'Don't blame me' inherent in the idea of inborn defect. Most especially, as with the case of the nine-year-old kid in foster care, the idea that something is biologically wrong with the children allows the state to divert attention from a system of social cruelty, and reduces the chance that the greater society will bother with action for change" (Armstrong, 1993, p. 167).

Addiction

Some of the newer thinking is linking addiction to a prior stress experience for the organism (person). Therapist John Omaha in California says there has been a traumatic insult to the person, which results in a compromised resilience. This compromised resilience leads the person to self-medicate with substances. Omaha says the neural networks have been co-opted by trauma. This takes place throughout this limbic system. Standard drug and alcohol treatments work with the neo-cortex.

Omaha says many addicts are unable to protect themselves from the intrusiveness of others. They do not have solidly established interpersonal boundaries. His clinic is having success using the new affective therapies to strengthen their clients. A detoxification is the first step for these clients. They cannot process feelings they are not feeling directly.

Dr. Omaha identifies contextual traumas as part of etiology in addiction. Poor parenting may be more of a problem for one child in the same family than for another. The "set-point" for resilience is different for each child. The trauma can be a "withhold." This means that the parent was silent or avoidant, and did not give the love and open support the child needed. This person may struggle all of his life to obtain the "withhold" from others, who will not know his history or understand his plight. Of course, there are self-healing mechanisms operant with each child; otherwise we would all be psychotic.

Families are not perfect. Omaha compares very poor parenting to pouring toxic chemicals early into the child's "stream of life." The child needs to accomplish difficult developmental tasks. The early toxicity makes it much more difficult. All of Erik Erikson's developmental stages are affected.

Omaha maintains the later addiction re-enacts the emotional wounding the person originally suffered. He claims to be able to tell at what stages, and by which parent, the child was wounded, by the client's later drug of choice and the way his addiction "drama" plays out.

Nathaniel Branden on Addiction

"When we become addicted to stimulants, we are avoiding the exhaustion or depression they are intended to mask. Whatever else may be involved in a particular case, what is always involved is the avoidance of consciousness. Sometimes what is avoided are the implications of a lifestyle that requires stimulants to be sustained.

"To the addict, consciousness is the enemy…If I recognize that I am in a relationship that is destructive to my dignity, ruinous for my self-esteem, and dangerous to my physical well-being, and if I nonetheless choose to remain in it, I must first drown out the voice of reason, fog my brain, and make myself functionally stupid. Self-destruction is an act best performed in the dark" (Branden, 1994, p. 81).

Fritz Perls on Addiction

Perls explains the cycle of shame experienced by addicts: "Freedom from Feeling of guilt and Anxiety are, according to a very primitive psycho-analytical conception, all that is required for the cure of a neurosis. They are indeed very unpleasant phenomena. The feelings of guilt (based upon the projected aggression) drive the 'sinner' into avoidance: 'I shall not do it again.'. But often enough, as in the case of chronic alcoholism, these feelings of guilt, though very deeply felt at the time, are not of any lasting consequence. They bribe the conscience or environment for the time being, but recede quickly enough into the background once the situation has changed-once the hangover has passed" (Perls, 1969, p. 68).

Other Addiction Issues

It is very difficult to motivate addicts. They no longer fear death, but only fear life lived without the substance. The addict is interested in getting high, getting over. There is a quality of revenge and selfishness in addiction. The client really "doesn't care." There is a large desire for complete oblivion present in addicts.

These clients can be helped with relationship. A good bond with the therapist is essential. Family bonds should be strengthened if possible. These clients need to learn how to take and give emotional comfort with close others. Good affective therapy will help them as well. Obviously, there are lacks in limbic system development. The client often has developed a grandiosity and a sense of entitlement. There is a narcissistic wound. The client is attempting to deal with a type of bravado, a defending "toughness." If the client has a love of dominance, it is to protect against the sense of inferiority.

At very young ages, the toddler is told "No." He must begin to understand others have desires; his will may have to accede to the will of another. It is a great shock to the developing child. If his world is kind and generally supportive, he will be able to tolerate this. If he is managed too harshly, or not taught these social laws at all, it can become very damaging. "I can't trust the people who take care of me to teach me the world in a kind way."

The addicted person needs spirituality and intimacy that is genuine. Our culture is not presently supporting these values. We see real intimacy repressed. Concomitantly, we see impersonal sex considered to be acceptable. Our times have created the perfect climate for high levels of addiction. And we do see high levels of addiction. The addicted person needs to learn and practice intimate, loving relationships. This is one reason groups like AA do have some effect on addiction. The addiction experience itself is highly anti-social.

The early relationships have been bad. "My past was stolen. How can I believe I have a future? How can I believe someone will love me in a genuine way? They never have."

The arts can be helpful. An addicted person is sensitive. Go further into the sensitivity with creative arts, music, painting, acting. A therapist can encourage a person to take the aggression he feels and channel it into building a good career or business that will support the self and a family. Harness that power and use it to build up the life. In the 1960's there was a poster that said: "Living well is the best revenge." Deepak Chopra talks about not removing a love or a comfort without replacing it with another.

The stress of life causes the client to begin to think obsessively of missing "x." X is something outside the person that he needs so badly that without it he cannot be complete. (This is magical thinking at its worst, of course. What John Omaha calls defective reality testing.) He must have x to be "ok." He then takes some compulsive, usually life damaging action, to get x. Even if he gets it, there is a letdown. The old EST training used to say: "You can never get enough of what you really don't want." The addict is actually looking for intimacy and spirituality.

Depression and guilt will follow the usage. Shame will then follow the guilt, beginning the cycle all over again, and leading back to stress. The person is looking for the limbic connectedness and trying to find his own most spiritual self. X was within him all along. Helping him see this is the job the therapist must do.

At the teen drug and alcohol rehabilitation hospital where I served my internship, I met D. He was a tall, good-looking boy of sixteen years of age from Philadelphia. He was a musician. He was so addicted to cocaine that even his heart stopping, causing him to faint, did not faze him. His family had been so indifferent in the past. D. told me of jumping off one of the bridges in Philadelphia to commit suicide. When he actually hit the water, he decided he did want to live. He swam furiously to shore. When he arrived home, wet, exhausted, sad and embarrassed, no one really cared to hear his story. What does that do to a boy's limbic system?

On Death and Dying

Our emotions are three years old. We don't care why anyone left us. All we know is that they left us. We are never ready, three years of age or thirty years of age. Why did this happen? Wasn't I a good enough person to make you stick around for me. We recognize these feelings are not rational and can be somewhat ashamed of them. The more unfinished business we have with the person, of course, the more painful the loss. Standard therapy techniques like the wrong-hand letter can be very helpful.

What was left unsaid? What was the worst thing about the death? What was given, not received? Trauma reprocessing will help someone in mourning.

Can Government Force People To Act In Their Best Interest? Public Health Dilemma/Limbic System Answer

In mental health, and in physical health, the question is increasingly asked in public health forums, how does the society get a population to act in a responsible manner? Because I have worked so much in the public mental health system, and we need families to be more responsible across the board in how they parent, this question is of great interest to me. We are increasingly learning how closely related we all actually are. If a depressed addict in New York City has drug resistant tuberculosis and won't treat it, it's my problem if I ride the subway with him. If a partner will not be honest about sexually transmitted diseases he is carrying, it could be my problem. If a juvenile is poorly treated in a system, and violently attacks someone on the street, it could be my problem. Financially speaking, personal behavior that harms any individual, even the self, creates financial problems for all of us.

So how do we get a population to act in a responsible manner? I'm convinced we can't. But if the right treatment is applied, and an individual's limbic system calms, he will himself make life-affirming choices.

This issue was identified and edified in a New York Times article, "Flirting with Suicide." Treatment people need to understand we will not succeed with 5 cents worth of behavior therapy as our only skill. There are complex reasons why people do what they do. And there are always reasons.

An article in The New York Times addressed issues of gay culture, but the psychology behind it can be extrapolated to understand all personal behavior that does not, on its surface, appear to be self-supportive. Yet psychology tells us people are seeking more comfort and support, in a successful or unsuccessful way, all of the time: "Getting people to change their private behavior for the public good, or even for their own well-being, has been a chronic national problem. Recent reports - much politicized this election season - show that drug use by teen-agers, after a period of steady decline, more than doubled between 1992 and 1995. Highly visible efforts to combat the problem of 'children having children' haven't worked either: 4 out of 10 American women become pregnant by the time they reach age 20-almost a million teenagers a year. Indeed, despite decades of effort, there is no clear consensus on what kinds of interventions even make a difference. Prescriptive, authoritarian campaigns like Just Say No may be effective in certain already-motivated populations, but they virtually repel those who most need addressing. And even if successful interventions are found, they tend to stop working long before anyone is willing to give them up.

"How cost is measured is the crux of the problem. Our current notions of public health are based on old, even ancient, models. Developed to contain everything from the plague to polio, classical interventions targeted more cohesive and tractable societies, and made less intrusive demands. Cover your nose and mouth when sneezing. But how do you 'do public health' (as public health people like to say) in a democracy? How do you weigh individual liberty against statistical risk? And what happens when the behavior in a question isn't a sneeze but part of a person's deepest core of identity? What if it's something he profoundly enjoys and doesn't want to give up?

"When a natural drive like sex gets tangled in unintended and even tragic results, public health is at its worst. 'Moralistic slogans and intervention programs based unrealistically on no-sex vows do not reduce teen pregnancy or sexual activity, ' says Gloria Feldt, president of the Planned Parenthood Federation of America. 'In fact, there have been studies that show they may actually increase the desire of teen-agers to experiment: to find out what it is they've been told to say not to. And then because they haven't been given the tools with which to experiment safely-and because they've been told that they are bad people if they prepare-the likelihood of pregnancy only goes up. Basically such programs don't work, ' she concludes, 'because ignorance is not bliss.'" (Green, 1996, p. 40).

This article also quotes Berkeley psychologist Walt Odets: "For the last few years, Odets has insisted on a re-evaluation of the entire effort - a call to arms with implications for all public health campaigns. In a recent book, in impromptu jeremiads and in a series of withering articles (one of them called 'The Fatal Mistakes of AIDS Education'), he has argued that prevention organizations have failed even the basic requirements of a sustainable initiative: to identify appropriate target audiences, provide them with accurate information and respect their right to weigh risk against benefit according to their own values. In doing so, he concludes, the groups have been guilty of ignoring the deepest root of gay men's unsafety: the psychological root, what they feel" (Green, 1996, p. 41-42).

A gentleman quoted in the article explained the situation as follows: "'Maybe I'm an extreme case, ' he continues, 'but I've met plenty of people like me. Go down Santa Monica Boulevard and look in the bars: it's lost people. And people like us don't pay any attention to the posters and ads. Don't they get it's hard to be safe? Think of the situation if you're looking to meet someone. You have to put away a lot of alcohol in the first place, just to get up the nerve, and then your reasoning is off. Last time, I was so toasted, I remember the room spinning. Luckily I passed out so nothing happened. But you can't blame it all on alcohol either. It's something within you that makes you go on these binges. You remember what it feels like when somebody wants you: you're a god. And then it's over and you're a heel again. Alcohol is a tool to free yourself to destroy yourself if you already want to. And no poster is going to solve that" (Green, 1996, p. 43).

Once again, we are seeing two recurring themes of this book: you can never get enough of what you really don't want, people are actually longing for a healing of their activated limbic systems, and the huge role of discouragement in clients: "But where are the rest of us supposed to learn how to love right? Maybe I did it wrong, but I wanted to experience happiness. Isn't that what we all want? Someone who's there for you, even if just for a moment? . . . Most prevention efforts have been based on risk-elimination, rather than risk reduction', he tells me during another of our many talks over the course of a year. 'But the question is whether one ever eliminates risk for things that are valuable. As a society, we do all kind of things that may or may not be in the interest of our long-term health because we consider them important. We weigh the risk against the value.'" (Green, 1996, p. 40).

The article goes on to say that: "In this main trait, Mark is exactly like most gay men I spoke to about unsafe sex: he refuels himself over and over not so much from a love of life itself but as from an apparently bottomless reservoir of hope for the companionship that makes life worth it" (Green, 1996, p. 55).

This type of longing and imagined need is what drives behavior in other populations who create risk: co-dependent parents who will neglect and risk their children, people involved in addictions, people who will not care for their own physical health. The person's careless behavior is also a kind of protest against the cruelties of life: When life is good to me and worthwhile, then I will do the right things. Until then, forget it. We need affective work, to click on the right folder, to help these clients.

References

Allport, G. (1954). The Nature of Prejudice. Boston: Beacon Press.

Armstrong, L. (1993). And They Call It Help. New York: Addison-Wesley.

Branden, N. (1994). Six Pillars of Self-Esteem. New York: Bantam Books.

Chernin, M. (1985). The Hungry Self. New York: Harper and Row.

Deikman, A. (1994). The Wrong Way Home. Boston: Beacon Press.

Fireside, H. (1992). The Grieving Child. New York: Simon and Schuster.

Green, J. (1996, September 15). Flirting With Suicide. The New York Times. Page 40-55.

Kohn, A. (1993). Punished By Rewards. New York: Houghton Mifflin.

Kutner, L. (1993, July 22). Petty Crime Can Be A Phase Or A Predictor. The New York Times. Section C, Page 10.

Perls, F. (1969). Ego Hunger & Aggression. New York: Random House.

CHAPTER FIFTEEN: BARRIERS TO TREATMENT

There are many blocks to treatment, many reasons why a person might not want to get well. Continuing into adulthood with a poor self-image has many pay-offs.

Even looking at fears is frightening for people. I think many people feel they have just barely glued themselves together, and the bond is very tenuous; they can't risk pulling at it. They will finally collapse altogether. Change is always frightening for all of us. What will we do with all of the time we free up if we are well?

Pay-offs:
I don't have to be responsible.
People can't ask too much of me.
I can punish people in my life, in a distorted way.
I like the righteous "I'm right and you're wrong" feeling.
Is there a guarantee if I try it will all work out for me?
I like to feel sorry for myself.
If I should feel happy, it's only a matter of time until I "crash?"
Why risk the disappointment?
I can control others with my self-pitying attitudes.
They can see what they made of me.

Additional blocks to health are that we are hoping someone else will do it all for us. This internal martyr is the only steady support I've ever had. How can I face life without this internal martyr? If I do risk change and it's too stressful, I will "unravel" completely. I've already forgiven these other people too often already. I want to stay stuck.

Francine Shapiro, who developed EMDR, adds that if we obtain wellness we may have to confront individuals or situations we have been afraid of dealing with. We may become attached to the therapist and fear wellness means we will lose one of the few good relationships we've ever had. The person may fear he is being disloyal to his parents if he looks at their behavior or becomes too unlike them. It may be a betrayal of the parental injunctions to not feel too well: don't surpass me. We may fear (rightly so) that, if I get strong, I'll have to leave a relationship I know is bad for me.

All of these blocks are false images. We are what we think, say, and do, and that changes each day. We are always changing. Each day is different, our "persona" is actually always in flux.

I've seen people ask for a treatment provider and then hope we don't know what we are doing. They will tell us "I hate my life now, but I'm too afraid of change. I can't face the unknown."

If we become strong enough, all of us can benefit from forgiving our parents. They made many mistakes and had a great deal of unfair power over us for a number of years. We were very vulnerable and they may not have been good to us. We can benefit from understanding their frailties and what forces shaped them. Knowledge of the parents and their original families can help us increase empathy for them. We can gain compassion for ourselves by studying young children we see in the environment or early pictures of ourselves. How open and lovely we once were.

Some cognitive steps in forgiveness of ourselves should be done. We can acknowledge we wasted a number of years being angry, or poor, or emotionally weak. That's the level of knowledge we had at that time. We can't get the time back but we need not be victimized further by these losses and errors in consciousness. Good affective work that works with the limbic brain can help with self-forgiveness. Sometimes, following some healing work, a person is simply left with a feeling of chagrin. I'm embarrassed I let myself down like this. I didn't need to go through this. It wasn't necessary. The WORST thing we can do to ourselves is let the embarrassment keep us from cutting our losses and making changes NOW. Many people feel even they themselves are not worth the continued, sustained effort healing will require of them, and that is sad.

The early stages of treatment involve continuously working through the blocks to change. Keep identifying them with the client and helping him tell the truth.

According to Rian McMullin, additional fears can be:
"It is easier not to change
I would have to change too many other things.
I won't let anybody tell me what to do.
I shouldn't have to work hard to change. It should happen quickly without a great deal of effort." (McMullin, 1986, p. 279).

Arthur Janov explains how change can optimally occur: "Defenses yield only to internal connection, never to external attack" (Janov, 1991, p. 160)

A person has made an investment in his defense. To be stripped of them is a dramatic experience.

Issues of Transference and Countertransference

Many clinicians attempt to "blow through" these issues and pretend they do not exist. Of course, in any relationship, one person is affected by his response to the other, and vice versa. An entire and excellent book could be written on transference issues, but here I will highlight some basics.

The Clinician Identifies Too Much With the Child

Sometimes the clinician finds himself solely in the child's corner. I have seen this often in foster care work. Perhaps he experienced some of the same things the child has experienced. This must be monitored by a supervisor. Perhaps the clinician needs treatment before he can deal with these issues. It is never helpful to approach anything with our judgements leading us. Identifying too much with the child can create a serious imbalance. There is jealousy if we replace the parent or shame the parent by "doing it better." Additionally, some day we must leave. We should transfer our skills to the parent, who is in the child's life. By allowing jealousy to fester with the parent, we increase the likelihood this parent will sabotage the treatment. I tell clients we are only the "hired help" and will never be as important in their lives as their loved ones. In the course of long careers, treatment people will see many reprehensible behaviors. It is vital to treat the spirit within the person and recognize we are just viewing their bad programming. If we can take some history from the parent, it is important for our understanding of the parent. Sometimes seeing a picture of that parent as a young child can be helpful to raise our empathy for the person. It is also easier to come in and deal with the child for a few hours, but the parent does have the difficulty day-in and day-out task of caring for that child and it can be very trying. It can be easy for us to look the hero.

The Clinician Identifies Too Much With the Parent

We have found many therapists will take the parent's side because it is easier, especially if a clinician really doesn't know how to do treatment and effect change. Therapists will sit and chat with the parent just to fill up the time. It is easier to take the parent's side, especially if you fear the parent. The parent has the power in the world. The parent can complain to your boss or the referral source. The child is unlikely to do so. This unfortunate dynamic can play out in marital therapy as well, with the therapist mollifying the more aggressive partner. Even in Sigmund Freud's era, the economic clout of the adults seems to have affected treatment. Psychologist Jeffrey Masson's excellent book, The Assault on Truth: Freud's Suppression of the Seduction Theory, details how Freud reversed himself. In fear of retaliation from powerful Victorian abusers (similar to today's False Memory lobbyists) he retracted his theory that clients had been sexually abused and claimed the women so desired the sexual relationships they fanaticized about them and then were ill because they suffered the effects of fantasies. In fact, the women exhibited the type of Post Traumatic Stress Disorder we see today is sexual abuse victims.

In private practice the parent is paying the practitioners. The parent tells the therapists most of the case history. The child is lucky if he get his "two cents" in. Sadly, the incentive can be to not aggravate the parent, to not dig too deeply and continue collecting the fee. Obviously, many good treatment people will tell the truth and risk getting fired, and, indeed, do get fired.

I deeply appreciate working in the public sector. Our treatment is voluntary for the family and we have often been fired, but we are never required to "skew" our opinions over financial and political concerns. The county where we have worked gets the credit for this and they do have good integrity. In the state of Pennsylvania, our clients, regardless of income, get the best treatment available to a child of any income level. No treatment in the private sector is better, or less likely to show bias. We are very proud of this in our unit.

Dealing with Difficult Clients

In sessions, if the client cannot settle down, and it doesn't feel as though the session will be productive, give the client back a bit of power. End the session by saying gently, "I'm a good therapist, but I don't think I can help you right now. You're so angry. I don't think I can be effective." And give it a week's break. Always allow an angry client to "save face" whenever possible. For so many males, extreme anger is the only emotion they feel allowed to express. The anger is actually fear, the one most unacceptable male emotion. Challenge angry clients to look at the real fears beneath the anger. If you weren't blowing off steam and very angry, what would you be feeling?

Sometimes a walk or an exercise like using the Gestalt feelings ball can interrupt a mood and allow a session to take place. I will usually offer affective work with silence on both sides, if that's what the client can tolerate. I'll just use the tapping.

If you are also dealing with an addiction in the client, consider the transference issues that are taking place. How does the client see you? Usually in some way as an authority figure. The authority figure makes only a small "leap" to become a punisher. Remember that the addiction itself indicated disorders in interpersonal relationships. Watch for ways in which the client will test the relationship.

The client may seem to be compliant and loving and try to seduce and manipulate you. Continue to think of yourself as a caring technician who is trying to do a job.

Transference issues can get very tricky. The client may use hate and anger. (He's really asking: do you really care for me? Or do you see me for the money? To what degree can I "try" you and have your caring still?) The client may try to make the therapy impossible because of his unconscious fears of change.

The therapeutic relationship will feel odd to some clients. It may be the first time the client experienced caring without sex being involved. So much coercion and manipulation goes on in sexual exchanges he may not believe there is a more simple way to obtain emotional care. The clinician can mitigate cynicism if he is skillful. Hopefully, he can teach the client how to be loving enough that he learns to obtain emotional care from others who are in his life-without sex or coercion. Emotional diseases are diseases of NEGOTIATION SKILLS.

Not every client is a "fit" for every therapist. I don't see any shame in referring someone out to another therapist if the person's needs are not something I am good at meeting or there is some interpersonal problem.

References

Janov, A. (1991). <u>The New Primal Scream.</u> Wilmington, DE: Enterprise Publishing.

McMullin, R. (1986). <u>Handbook of Cognitive Therapy Techniques.</u> New York: W.W. Norton and Company.

CONCLUSION

Treatment work is so very satisfying. I'm convinced that when a clinician is effective he never feels "burned out." Of course at times people are hostile to good treatment, extremely hostile to difficult truths. Treatment people need regular vacations, diversions, and supportive relationships of their own.

When I was younger I wanted very badly to become a famous painter. I was trained in a very good school of fine art. I still love the visual arts. Yet I now think of what I'm doing in treatment as a living work of art. Someone who becomes very well after having been very ill walks differently, speaks very differently, holds his body very differently. The person's face is different, forever after, different. It is very exciting. A living, breathing sculpture - a work of art.

We now have superb tools to help clients reprocess old traumatic experiences and renegotiate their relationships. Some very strange mental health treatments have been used by supposedly expert physicians in earlier times. People were "helped" with castration, trepanning (drilling into the skull), injections of horse blood, ingesting powdered "unicorn horns, " electroshock, ice picks inserted into the eye socket, confinement with snakes, radical temperature exposures, physician induced epilepsy and physician induced insulin shock treatments. We now have many new, effective treatments to help people. I firmly believe almost every patient who is willing to work hard himself, and has a well-trained clinician, can have a good life, free of inordinate fears and anxieties.

Mahatma Gandi said to not be angry with our children, but to allow for their ignorance and that we should play with them and love them..

Rabbi Moshe Leib told us to act as if there were no God, as if there were only one person in all the world who could help this man- only you yourself.

And from <u>Leaves of Grass</u>: "This is what you should do: love the earth and sun and the animals, despise riches, give alms to everyone that asks, stand up for the stupid and crazy, devote your income and labor to others, hate tyrants, argue not concerning God, have patience and indulgence toward the people, take off your hat to nothing known or unknown or to any man or number of men...re-examine all you have been told at school or church, or in any book, dismiss what insults your own soul, and your very flesh shall be a great poem" (Whitman, 1855, Preface).

References

Fisher, L. (1962). <u>The Essential Gandi.</u> New York: Random House.
Whitman, W. (1855). <u>Leaves of Grass.</u>

ABOUT THE AUTHOR

Nancy Marshall studied Fine Art and English at Virginia Commonwealth University when it was part of the College of William and Mary. She obtained her Master's Degree in the Pennsylvania state system. She has worked as a psychotherapist since 1985 and lives in Pennsylvania. She currently supervised a Family-Based Mental Health Treatment Unit of three teams of therapists. She also maintains a private practice and works with Healing Work in Allentown, Pennsylvania. She is an expert in trauma treatment and is certified to use EMDR. *Why Family Therapy Doesn't Work* is the result of many years of experience in family therapy. The book is dedicated to all of those of us who have found it difficult to love someone and to young therapists who would like a more inventive, eclectic approach to healing and want to be more successful.

Ms. Marshall is licensed in Pennsylvania and New Jersey.